Storm Cycle 2013
The Best of Kind of a Hurricane Press

Edited by: A.J. Huffman
and April Salzano

Cover Art: "Red Skies in the Morning" by A.J. Huffman

Copyright © 2014 A.J. Huffman

All rights reserved. Except for brief quotations in critical articles or reviews, no part of this book may be reproduced in any manner without prior written permission from the publisher:

Kind of a Hurricane Press
www.kindofahurricanepress.com
kindofahurricanepress@yahoo.com

CONTENTS

	Thank You from the Editors	3
	From the 2013 Editor's Choice Contest Winners	
Barbara Bald	My Mother's Tongue	7
Kim King	ROYGBIV	9
Daniel Meltz	Just Outside of Bowler City	10
Patricia L. Goodman	Rescue	12
Denise R. Weuve	When to Tell Him That You Love Him	13
	From the 2013 Pushcart Prize Nominees	
Mike Cluff	Border Crossings	17
Jacqueline Markowski	Ashes	18
Rex Sexton	Gift Wrapped	20
Laura Grace Weldon	Why the Window Washer Reads Poetry	21
Serena Wilcox	Nocturnal Syllables	22
Gabrielle Williams	My Body is an Orphanage	23
	From The Anthologies	
Pamela Ahlen	Seascape	27
Mary Jo Balistreri	Christmas Engagement	29

James Bell	Angel at the Top of the Christmas Tree	30
Carly Berg	In the Cards	31
Michael H. Brownstein	The Color of Sound in the City	34
Candace Butler	Narcissus	35
Christine Clarke	The Kiss	36
	Requiem for Icarus	37
Suzanne C. Cole	The Last Letter Ever Written	38
Susan Dale	A Wild Gallop Across the Heavens	40
	My Homing Pigeon Heart	43
Cassandra Dallett	Losing Feathers	45
Jessica de Koninck	This Boardwalk Life	47
Darren C. Demaree	Without Thread, Here, We Are Connected to Everything	48
Andrea Janelle Dickens	Hatteras Evacuation	49
Neil Ellman	Metamorphosis	52
Alexis Rhone Fancher	Staying Put	53
Elysabeth Faslund	Sun and Sand Flipside	55
Joan Fishbein	Before	56

Trina Gaynon	*Sandsurfing*	58
Jessica Gleason	*Prologue: Alternate Version*	60
Marilou Goodwin	*Choose Unwisely*	61
Ray Greenblatt	*Christmas Dawn*	64
John Grochalski	*Poem to the Asshole Blasting Angry Birds on his iPad*	65
Marilyn Hammick	*Portraits of the Unseen*	66
Ed Higgins	*Astrobiography*	67
Liz Hufford	*Echoes of the Game*	68
Ken L. Jones	*Jammed Transmissions*	69
Judith Katz	*Green Sky at Night*	70
Claire Keyes	*Einstein at the Beach*	72
Michael Magee	*Solzhenitsyn at the Beach*	73
Ally Malinenko	*Astronaut*	74
Jacqueline Markowski	*On the Coast*	75
	Intelligent Design	77
Joan McNerney	*Arctic Flurries*	78
Karla Linn Merrifield	*The Properties of Rock*	79
Jane Miller	*Rosamund the Fair*	80

Bradley Morewood	*Space*	83
Wilda Morris	*Incarnation*	84
Loretta Oleck	*The Synaesthete*	86
Jeffrey Park	*On Display*	88
Faith Paulsen	*Quiet Edges*	89
Andrew Periale	*Untitled*	90
Freya Pickard	*Aspects*	91
Winston Plowes	*White Vessel with Inverted Triangle*	92
henry 7. reneau, jr.	*Red*	93
Kirby Snell	*I Have the Blooms*	94
Russell Streur	*Astrology*	95
Christine Tsen	*Jawing*	97
Mal Westcott	*Miro Paints the Shortness of Breath*	99
	Dream Caused by Sleep Apnea a Second Before Opening a Pomegranate Soda	100
John Sibley Williams	*The Moon is a Body*	102
Martin Willitts, Jr.	*Picasso's Blue Paint*	103
Robert Wynne	*Reflection: After the Great Wave*	104

Ron Yazinski	*Off Key West, Hemingway Sails with Homer*	105
	Research and Development	106
Dana Yost	*A Light of Their Own*	109
Ed Zahniser	*The Somatic Art Critic*	110

From the Journals

Shaquana Adams	*To Cheating Ex Boyfriends*	113
Alek Barkats	*untitled*	114
	sleePMapnia	115
Jon Bennett	*The Things*	116
	3 Fish in a Pool	117
Joop Bersee	*Weightless*	118
	Damnation	119
Abra Bertman	*Smoke*	120
Shinjini Bhattacharjee	*Me O'Clock*	121
Sara Bickley	*untitled*	122
Brenton Booth	*Pinched*	123
Bob Brill	*Silence in the Woods*	124
Michael H. Brownstein	*A Body's Language is Sometimes Written in Latin*	126
	A Chain of Days	127

J.J. Campbell	Slice of Utopia	128
Theresa A. Cancro	The Mermaids Won't Tell	129
	Leaves	130
	Seething Blue	131
Valentina Cano	Peace	132
Arthur Carey	A Wedding Gift to Remember	133
Fern G.Z. Carr	Not Enough	136
J.R. Carson	Glucose	137
Joseph James Cawein	Warm	139
Martin Cohen	Drizzle	140
Corey Cook	untitled	141
	Leafing Out	142
Larry Crist	The Frenzy of the Red Berry	143
Philip Dacey	Theme and Variations	145
Susan Dale	Passions (haiku string)	146
Cassandra Dallett	The Funny Thing Is	147
	Found a Pawn Slip	149
Mohana Das	Hyacinths in the Gutter:	151
William Davies, Jr.	Discovery	152

	Spring Contest	153
	Blink	154
Jim Davis	*Temperance*	155
Darren C. Demaree	*Emily as a Lake, a Lilac*	157
	Adoration #90	158
Jacob Dodson	*Pick-Up Haiku*	159
	Untitled	160
Janet Doggett	*Film Noir*	161
J.K. Durick	*Trial Separation*	162
	Playing at It	163
	Dog	164
Ann Egan	*Soldier Leaves*	165
Neil Ellman	*Elephants Remember*	166
	Fish	167
Kristina England	*The Distance You Can Traverse in a Minute*	168
	Split Ends	170
Alexis Rhone Fancher	*Haiku for My Beloved*	173
	How the Artist Sees the World	174

Jennifer Fauci	*A Quarter Past Time to Move On*	175
Zachary Fechter	*Un Blodymary*	176
	Rainmaker	177
Sharon Fedor	*Perigee*	178
Ryan Quinn Flanagan	*Memory*	179
Sarah Flint	*The Time Witch and the Forgetting Wizard*	180
Kenyatta Jean-Paul Garcia	*And Tracked*	181
	Fading Comes Easily	183
Allison Grayhurst	*We Sorrowed Far When the Sky Tore*	184
	Fill the Ghost with Upward Rejoicing	186
John Grey	*Dead Bulls Poem*	187
Tom Gribble	*Study 16*	188
Judy Hall	*A Poem from the Editors*	189
Christopher Kenneth Hanson	*Staid, The Night*	191
	A Fictional Heist	192
Linnea Wortham Harper	*A Grievance*	193
	Chilled	194

	He Met Somebody at a Conference	195
Jim Harrington	Waiting for the Storm to Pass	196
Dawnell Harrison	Indigo Blue Night	199
	Train Wreck	200
	Motherless	201
Rick Hartwell	Color Codes	202
	Sneaky	203
	After the Talk	204
Tom Hatch	Scraps of Paper Her Nights of Christ's Shirt	205
	Tapestry	207
Damien Healy	Judgment Day	208
	Beyond CPR	209
Ruth Hill	'Round Round Rodin	210
Kevin M. Hibshman	Narcissus	212
	Cat Goddess	213
H. Edgar Hix	Virgone	214
Lynn Hoffman	The Intelligent Design Café	215
Sue Neufarth Howard	untitled	216

	untitled	217
	untitled	218
S.E. Ingraham	*Nigh Time*	219
Jason Irwin	*Big Toe*	220
M.J. Iuppa	*Household*	221
	Temptation in Standard Time	222
	Concurrence	223
Diane Jackman	*Moor*	224
Miguel Jacq	*Frost*	226
Bill Jansen	*Damnit Roy*	227
	McSea	229
	Front Page	230
Michael Lee Johnson	*California Summer*	231
	I Am Looking for Something	232
	Empty Branch Tree	234
Ryan Kauffman	*Sunset in Morningview, KY*	236
Yasmin Khan	*untitled*	238
Maureen Kingston	*Found Poem: The Art (of the) Come-On: An Overheard Emoticon*	239

	The Un-Found Poems	240
	Sym-bi-otico: A Notorious Liberal Bastion Prepares for the Fall Semester (When God Closes a Door He Opens a Window)	241
Steve Klepetar	*Somewhere*	242
John Kross	*My Forte*	244
	(St) Ben(edict)	245
Craig Kyzar	*Wires Stripped Bare*	248
Heller Levinson	*Corner of Abscess & Silk*	249
Glenn Lyvers	*Kazuya Yamamoto*	250
David Macpherson	*How to Be Calm*	252
Donal Mahoney	*Chauvinist's Manifesto*	254
	Study in Fidelity	256
Ally Malinenko	*Photograph, Age Eleven*	257
	The Car Accident, 1995	259
Denny E. Marshall	untitled	260
	Fifteen Word Title	261
Alessandra Mascarin	*I Had a Dream and I Was There*	262
David McLean	*After History Ends*	263

Joan McNerney	*Virtual Love*	264
	untitled	265
Jim Meirose	*The Call*	266
Karla Linn Merrifield	*Night is a Rarer Place*	268
	Liver	269
Les Merton	*Life in the Shell*	270
	End	271
	In the Garden	273
John Miatech	*untitled*	274
James Mirarchi	*Zoom*	275
Mark J. Mitchell	*Technicolor*	276
Suchoon Mo	*Haiku after Santoka*	277
M.V. Montgomery	*Sound and Sense*	278
	Cold Hard Flash	279
	Dream Jobs	282
Afzal Moolla	*The Dilution of Memory*	285
Bradley Morewood	*The Snake in the Pool*	286
Erik Moshe	*Mesoamerica*	287
Christina Murphy	*Summer Reflections*	288
Tendai R. Mwanaka	*Love Can Be*	290

Adam Natali	*The Mighty Eagle*	291
Rees Nielsen	*The Karl Rove of Checkers*	293
ayaz daryl nielsen	*untitled*	294
Alex Nodopaka	*untitled*	295
Agholor Leaonard Obiaderi	*Seeking*	296
	Haunted	298
Timothy Ogene	*Homeland*	299
Turk Oiseau	*The Gift*	300
Loretta Oleck	*Cicada Shell (haiku string)*	301
Mary Orovan	*untitled*	302
Al Ortolani	*Lorca Deep Fries a Turkey*	303
Derek Osborne	*Nineteen in '72*	304
James Owens	*Late in the Year*	305
Jeffrey Park	*Air Passage*	306
	Animal Instincts	307
Lisa Pellegrini	*Bird Nests*	308
Andrew Periale	*untitled*	309
Perry L. Powell	*Our Collections*	310
John Pursch	*Mnemonic Peacock*	311

	Aching Aloud	313
Jenny Qi	*The Magnificent Capacity of Two Fireflies*	314
Stephen V. Ramey	*Beggar*	315
Niall Rasputin	*Sometimes*	317
	Mourning Walk	318
Chris Redfern	*Snipers in the Sun*	319
Laura Rojas	*When You Cross the Street Like a Sailor Breathing Underwater*	320
John Roth	*A Geisha Reminisces Over an Illicit Love Affair*	321
	Dehydration	323
	Quench	324
Sy Roth	*Hirsute Fantasy*	325
	A Bifurcated Road	326
	Avatars Dissolve on the Wind	327
Walter Ruhlmann	*Three Times Thirteen – Black Balloon, The Kills*	328
Weldon Sandusky	*1515 13th Street*	329
M.A. Schaffner	*The Point of Picking Berries*	330

	It All Comes Down to Investment Strategy	331
Carl Scharwath	untitled	332
Ken Seide	Memory Pillow	333
Dr. Ehud Sela	It Was There	334
Andreyo Sen	The Absence of Silence	335
	Village by the Sea	336
H. Alexander Shafer	Hands	337
Matthew Sharos	In the Absence Of	339
Tom Sheehan	Hawk, Poised	340
Felino A. Soriano	Of Trumpet 1	341
	Delineated Angles this Odonate	342
	On (a) Reacting to Her	343
Dr. Smita Sriwastav	She Wore a Marigold in Her Hair	344
	She Murmured Her Against the Silence	346
	Harlequin Whispers of Night Sky	347
Melissa Steinle	Father May I	348
Leilanie Stewart	Landmass	349
	Snowball Effect	350

	Twenty Questions	351
Emily Strauss	*One Hundredth Meridian*	352
	The Wind Hits	354
Jason Sturner	*Promise of an Eagle, to a Friend*	355
André Surridge	*untitled*	357
A.g. Synclair	*Exposed*	358
	Penang	359
	I Was Just Thinking	360
Marianne Szlyk	*The River Always Captures Me*	361
	Marigold	363
Yermiyaho Ahron Taub	*Dialect in Abeyance*	364
Sarah Thursday	*Viscosity*	365
	Lies to Tell My Body	366
Josette Torres	*I Continue to Refuse the Role I am Given*	368
Chuch Von Nordheim	*untitled*	369
	untitled	370
Anthony Ward	*Affection*	371
	Playing on My Mind	372

Diane Webster	Blue Sky Dolphins	374
Eric A. Weil	Late October Soybeans	375
Kelley White	Morris's Magnetic Literary Stuffonmycat Haiku	376
	untitled	377
Serena Wilcox	Variations	378
Stephen Jarrell Williams	Burial	379
	Desert Flowers	380
Patrick Williamson	University Years	382
Martin Willitts, Jr.	Fishing in Silence	383
	untitled	385
Cherise Wyneken	Springing Forward	386
Ron Yazinski	Airbrushing	387
Tony Yeykal	The Oculist's Patient	389
Mantz Yorke	Black Hole	390
Dana Yost	The Lonely Stalk Their Front Room Windows at Night	392
Changming Yuan	The Chinese Painter and the Viewer	393
Bänoon Zan	Disarmament	394
Ali Znaidi	untitled	395

From The Editors

A.J. Huffman	*Killing for a Dream of Self-Preservation*	399
	Walking with Birds	400
	Of Adverbs and Misguided Affairs	401
	Conversation with an Uncooked Egg	402
	Fourth of July Haiku	403
April Salzano	*Shoveling the Trampoline*	404
	Battle at the Birdfeeder	405
	The Real Story	406
	Autism Haiku (haiku string)	407
	Assault by Baby	408
	Author Bios	411
	About the Editors	457

Thank You From The Editors

In lieu of an introduction, we wanted to take a moment to thank all of our brilliant authors from 2013. We have been blessed with an amazing amount of extraordinarily talented authors who deemed our journals and anthologies worthy of their wonderful work. This thank you extends not just to the authors who made the pages of this anthology, or even to the authors that made the pages of our other anthologies and online journals, but rather to all the authors who submitted their work to us. Accepted, rejected, chosen as standouts, at the end of the day without any of you, none of our hard work would matter at all. Without the diligent work of these struggling artists, we would be a blank page on a screen or a book. So, for saving us from that horrific fate, we thank you. We hope to continue our relationship with all of you, and any and all new additions we can muster. We have an amazing year of projects planned for 2014. Hopefully, we will see you all again in the years to come.

*From The 2013
Editor's Choice Contest Winners*

My Mother's Tongue

She used to stick it out for me, displaying
the deep cleft down its middle, irregular bumpy sides
and tiny cracks like those on misfired porcelain.
She'd extend it, roll it into a long tight tube, then
flatten it to reveal its blotchy red surface.

We'd stand before the bathroom mirror, comparing
the hated old tongue to my young flawless, flat one
and I'd listen to her berate it and whatever else she saw
as her other imperfect features.

It was a tongue that could slice with Samurai precision.
Who the hell do you think you are? pierced phone lines
when my father's fishing buddies woke her at 4:00 am,
asking for Captain Joe.

Would you mind moving over? she'd hiss
at the churchgoer who refused to slide into the wooden pew,
causing me to cower in teenage humiliation.

The tongue had no respect for boundaries.
With words, *You didn't let him touch you, did you?*
or *Where does your boyfriend stay when he visits?*
it would pry into private areas where it had no place.

Mostly, her tongue would judge --
the friend who wore too many bracelets,
the spaghetti sauce that never tasted as good as hers.
You don't know how to dance, do you? she would notice
aloud.
The tongue always called a spade more than a spade.

I had planned to use my young tongue to spread rose petals,
to help polish those who wanted to see their own shine.
If my tongue flapped in unkindness, I hoped
it would be a butter knife rather than a sword --

Today, with my sixty-year old tongue extended to my dentist,
I learned I have what's called a geographical tongue.
The red splotches and tiny fissures of its surface resemble
Pangaea-like plates that react to spicy meals.

Remembering words, *I never asked her to be born.*
If you don't like it, go home, cruelties I once hurled
at my mother and others, I cringed when he said it,
It's hereditary, you know.
You have your mother's tongue.

                         -- Barbara Bald
                         (First Place Prize Winner)

ROYGBIV

The yellow bloomed a week after the biopsy --
blurring into the indigo and violet bruises, a dab
of cadmium paint, like in Matisse's *Woman with a Hat*,
her solemn, green-tinged face and down-turned mouth
glowered under a garish feather and baubled chapeau.
Her squared collar, like my cotton hospital gown,
over-sized and unadorned, concealed her inner wounds.
Mine were under a lacey bra, protected with steri strips
and bandages, but no artist was at the easel. Instead,
doctors weighed "high risk lesion" and "rare
in zero point zero four percent" with "prevalence
of early tubular carcinoma," while I balanced
a prism refracting white
light in Mr. Grant's seventh grade class,
reciting the colors of the spectrum, in order.

-- Kim King
(Second Place Prize Winner)

Just Outside of Bowler City

my first teacher was my father
a sarcastic figure in underpants
he taught me how to
idolize and instigate
my mother
ran from him

she brushed her hair till it bounced
she used
the hairbrush as a weapon
she loved
the smell of the future
but she never stepped into it

my sister showed me her workbook
a multiplication table and
spelling lists
she turned on cartoons
heckle and jeckle
two angry crows

she told me about her teachers at school
the teacher with the swinging can
the teacher with the blubbery neck
the one with the
swishing stockings
the one with the
tangerine lipstick

we shared a bedroom with a kidnap window
we stage-whispered at daybreak
biting the cream out of cookies

we broke bobby pins in two
and scratched every inch of a crap credenza

-- Daniel Meltz
(Third Place Prize Winner)

Rescue

On the wooded steps of a Nature Center
I find a plastic eye -- the flat kind

with the pupil that moves if you shake it.
It lies there staring. I imagine

the toy it came from, a teddy bear
perhaps, who now sees the world

in monovision. When my childhood
teddy's eyes wore off, Mom replaced them

with shoe buttons. He and I saw each other
differently then, grew accustomed.

After my husband died and I began
my climb from despair, I rescued Teddy

from the back of a dark drawer.
We cried.

-- Patricia L. Goodman
(Honorable Mention)

When to Tell Him That You Love Him

Wait
until he is in the kitchen
cleaning lunch dishes and you
are walking away.
Make sure the water runs heavy and loud.

Mouth the words
never daring to let the sound escape
as he leaves the table to pour
another cranberry
vodka
to keep you under.

Sign it distinctly
as he hunches over to check
the air in the tires
explaining for the 8th time
how you can do this yourself.

Etch it in the sky
when he is looking downstream
waiting for Salmon to hook on his line
so he can show you the dinner
you make him throw back.

Lock it away
in an old shoebox, fill it
with the paper bag he brought Dansville oranges
to you in. The one that said
"Don't touch. Just hers."

-- Denise R. Weuve
(Honorable Mention)

*From The 2013
Pushcart Prize Nominees*

Border Crossings

Cakewalking across the Ohio
dividing safe from death
every winter storm gets worse
fragments of nature's anger
grinding and pushing down the
hope that bubbles up
in any immigrant's soul
justice for none of color
kelp would never survive this far north
lynchings do
many, too many times over.

Nips, neverstopping, of arctic cold
overwhelm those who are weak
putting them under bloody ice floes
quickly, without qualms
remorse is a quality some people
seldom display to those who are not
their own
unless utility is rationalized via
viscious impluses burbling up
without compassion with
xylophones producing cacaphonies
yammering "repression, drawing and quartering, tar and
feathering" upward to the
zenith of haughty, horrible hate
always growing, mutating
beatitudes of the master's, master race's religions.

-- Mike Cluff
(August The Mind[less]Muse))

Ashes

In another life I was an avid stoner. My boyfriend, Paul, only knew other stoners. We went to a party once. Thick with THC and trying to appease Phthonos, my paranoid mind wove a tapestry: Paul had sent the quiet dude on the couch to flirt with me—to see if I would tell on him, to test my loyalty. Paul told me many times that he'd kill me if I ever cheated. The dude left the couch when the conversation slowed and I never saw him again. I spent at least an hour trying to remember the word "entrapment". I had the "trap" part but couldn't remember the rest.

Later we smoked a joint with the couple who lived there. He rolled it fat, leaving in all the seeds and stems. He said, through a thick Russian accent, that to truly love cannabis, one must accept and appreciate it all, a sentiment punctuated with the popping of a red hot seed which kamikaze-dove from the forest-for-the-trees-joint into the man's lap. *Cantárida*, he yelled. There was an eruption of laughter. Maybe he was from Mexico. From there I floated on a cloud of deeper appreciation for the interconnectedness of everything, even the nuts and bolts of weed. My thoughts meandered peacefully until his wife tugged at my cloud, beckoning me to a dark corner across the room. She dug through her oversized purse, pulling out rustic tampons and q-tips and denture cream while she searched for her treasure, which I hoped was eye drops or gum. Finally she pulled out a gallon sized ziplock bag.

It was half full of a white powder. I froze in place, afraid it was a felonious amount of something that might counteract this beautifully mellow high. I was right to be cautious. *My first husband,* she said. There was an hour of silence before I realized that she was finished with the sentence. I couldn't figure out how to say I was lost in the conversation. *It's him... His ashes. Here...* she said, clearly frustrated with my cognitive inabilities. She unzipped the bag, put it to my nose, willing me to smell the act of cremation. I pretended to inhale, moving my shoulders up above my drooping head. Still congratulating myself on a damn fine act of pantomime, I saw that she was frowning and disappointed. *Touch him.* After negotiating with the reality of what she'd just said, I lowered my hand below the zippered line of the opening of the bag and pretended to touch the contents. *No, like grab some. Pick him up.* Not yet satisfied, she pinched a thimble-sized amount by way of example. I tried not to do what she was asking of me. While my hand was in the bag, hovering over the ash like The Hindenburg, she pulled the bag up, into my hand. *There,* she said with a satisfied smile. I looked up, shocked, hoping maybe it was an earthquake that crashed my hand into her dead first husband's remains. That would've been so much easier.

Behind her I saw Paul walking toward us, looking curious, hurried. Believing it possible he might feel threatened, I quickly pulled my arm out of this poor dead man's burnt body. But my hand was covered in him. Up to my wrist. I had fisted the mother fucker! And now what? I was left with yet another awkward conundrum. Should I clap my hands together so that most of him would fall to the ground and then blow off the rest? Would that be considered rude in this type of situation? Should I wipe him on my shorts? Should I excuse myself and wash him off in the bathroom sink? What had she done with the thimble-full? If only I had paid attention. Typical me, always missing the details.

What *did* I do? I wish I could remember but I can't because suddenly my boyfriend grabbed my arm, hard and pulled me toward the door. I couldn't even utter a word, I barely had my footing. He dragged me to the car and drove us away furiously. At first I thought he was being noble, saving me from the horrible social predicament of what to do with a fist full of some chick's first husband's ashes. But he wasn't. He was pissed. He had received the report from the flirting couch-dude.

-- Jacqueline Markowski
(February Pound of Flash)

Gift Wrapped

Things tied with strings, or wrapped
with ribbons, my life, until the package
unraveled.
I married a dark-eyed girl, raised some
children. I lavished them in all the
nine-to-five amenities my blood, sweat
and tears could bring them – we were broke
a lot to sum it up, never broken.
Love, marriage, the baby carriage, OK
by me, both of us – our blue heaven shopping
at the seven-eleven. Anything beyond that
either flat left us or left us flat. We were
OK with that.
The great mysteries, God, existence, destiny,
were moonbeams lighting our home and
we left them alone content with the glow
they added to life in their own opague way.
Now the man who lives here isn't there,
not in his head or bed, upon the stair or
anywhere. The dark eyed girl is gone, maybe
to heaven, away from our blue one. Life
lingers on, she lingers on, some, in the
presence of the children whenever
I see them, which isn't very often.

-- Rex Sexton
(April Pyrokinection)

Why the Window Washer Reads Poetry

for Michael, who carried poems in his work shirt pocket

He lowers himself
on a seat they call a cradle, rocking
in harnesses strung long-armed
from the roof.

Swiping windows clean
he spends his day
outside looking in.

Mirrors refract light into his eyes
telescopes point down
photographs face away,
layers of dust
unifying everything.

Tethered and counterbalanced
these sky janitors hang,
names stitched on blue shirts
for birds to read.
Squeegees in hand they
arc lightly back and forth across
the building's eyes
descend a floor, dance again.

While the crew catches up
he pauses, takes a slim volume from his pocket
and balancing there,
36 stories above the street,
reads a poem or two
in which the reader is invariably placed
inside
looking out.

-- Laura Grace Weldon
(Poised in Flight Anthology)

Nocturnal Syllables

The body
turns tightly
under the shadow of trees,
the sky is lacerated
by lightning,
clouds withdraw slowly
there, a soft
crescent sickle
implanted in darkness
is surrounded by embers
of glinting
cold
lights

if you must die,
go quietly,
lie unchanging
swaddled in deep sleep,
death will die
a thousand times
before the end of the night,

this is what the wilderness looks like…

-- Serena Wilcox
(January Jellyfish Whispers)

My Body is an Orphanage

This is a California dream of Jack and the beach
of waking up in toothpick colored sand(s)
running to the shore and back.

There are salty billionaires in
southern California, in Newport Beach, in San Francisco
a memoir of the city resisting totality.

This is an entrance to the simplicity of his sauced body.
We have stopped eating.

***

Buffy the Vampire Slayer as a
metaphor for being in love
with musicians—
the effervescent groupie: an affair that I have dog-eared for
later.

I am uncertain of our verbal history
I am an anti-fact
I am hunting bears with confectioner's sugar
My body is a sovereign nation.
He is grand wizard he is svelte
He is an investment

This is a concrete documentary.
This is a pyramid song
like a glasshouse.

I am an ugly Christmas sweater
I am moving forward with my life I am becoming
ambidextrous
This was a series of empty events.
I am a sugar bowl a fire escape a telescope
I am immured

I am sand   paper
I am wet wood and pillars.

This is us revisiting our sandcastles.
We are folding over the love parts.

-- Gabrielle Faith Williams
(May Pyrokinection)

From the Anthologies

Seascape

At the edge of sea to shining
beneath the spacious sky,
the brotherhood of fishing poles and SCV's,
big beach covered in best buy,
sea filled with American Dreams.

*

Near the wrinkled rose
and the bench marked
Yet We But Borrow the Land
the artist paints pink stain sky,
a white daub of saltbox house,
smears of oil-slick tide.

*

Charlie builds castles on sand,
develops the shore
and offends the land,
his need to greed
persistent as the riptide sea.

*

She paddles past *Belinda's* bow,
the gull patrolling *Brenda's* stern,
paddles across the cove and skirts the stone bank –
paying homage to graying skiffs
clumped together like forgotten fishwives,
unnamed ladies bobbing mute, their secrets in repose.

*

We spend our lives
out of water,

fish treading
dryland shore.
Here at the sea
we've come home,
lungs to gills and arms to fins,
floating the sweet-salt sea
on pink rubber ducks,
green manatees.

-- Pamela Ahlen
(Of Sun and Sand Anthology)

Christmas Engagement

Betrothed during the night to winter
an oak twig displays
its glistening stone
against the plate glass window
its rosy hue of poinsettia red
beaming in the crystalline sun

> *-- Mary Jo Balistreri*
> *(Conversation with a Christmas Bulb Anthology)*

Angel at the Top of the Christmas Tree

They call
me
a fairy
as I hang
by a
wire
up here.

If they
call
me
a fairy
again
I will be
forced
to display
my darker
side
     and
pull a
wire
to fuse
the lights.

                -- James Bell
                (Conversation with a Christmas Bulb Anthology)

In the Cards

Shuffle cards a predetermined number of times. How many times? It doesn't say. I'll shuffle seven times, my lucky number. One, two... These cards are too big to shuffle right. Double it, then. Fourteen times. I was supposed to light a candle. There, a red candle, for love.

Choose the subject card. A card that stands for him. He's a Scorpio, it says that's... Cups. Damn, I was supposed to do this first. Now I'll have to shuffle again. He'd be five of cups, for the number of days he hasn't called. Or three, for me, him, and that Tanya bitch... I'll just do the Prince. Prince of Cups. Re-shuffle. Fourteen times. One, two...

Choose cards in order from the top of the deck. Lay them out in Celtic Cross formation, as shown.

Now...

Card 1 represents the situation. And it is the Strength Card. *Having the strength to bring opposing forces into agreement.* No, wait. The card was upside down. So it's the opposite of that. Why doesn't he call me back? Maybe what I heard isn't even true. He might be mad at me for something else. You never know. I hope he's okay. Even though his car was there, then it wasn't, doesn't mean he's okay. I'm calling the hospital again.

Card 2 represents what is influencing the situation- Nine of Swords. Where's that instruction booklet? Ah, there it is. *Torment from worries.* Yeah, no kidding. Even if it is true, I might forgive him. He could have been drunk, and is really sorry. He's afraid to answer me. That's very likely. He's afraid to face me, after his big mistake. Where's my cigarettes?

Card 3 represents the foundation of the issue. Six of Cups. Let's see... *Longing for the sweetness and innocence of the past. Happy home with children.* Oh yes, if only. I'd give anything.

These cards are speaking right to me. Amazing, really. People laugh at this stuff, but they don't know. I mean, did that card hit it on the nose or didn't it? Yes, it did. He's probably depressed. He probably didn't even do anything with the bitch. Depression runs in his family, after all, so it's not only me saying it.

Card 4 represents that which is passing away. Three of Cups. *Reason to celebrate, possibly a wedding.* A possible wedding passing away? Oh my God. Where's that lighter? Nevermind, I'll use the candle. I need a glass of wine. Ah, here we go, whiskey on the rocks. Wait. I hope it's that Tanya skank's plans that are passing away. It doesn't say *whose* hopes. If it's even true. Why won't he answer his phone? I bet he's miserable and depressed and afraid to face me. Especially after how I yelled on his voicemail. I shouldn't have yelled.

Card 5 represents what is on the questioner's mind. Three of Swords. *End of a love relationship.* The end. The end. Oh dear God, no. Nah, these cards are junk, it's only a carnival game and I'm being ridiculous. I need to go over there and straighten this out. Maybe he's home now.

Card 6 represents the influence now coming into play. Two of Cups. *A serious relationship.* But it's upside down. The opposite of that. Look at me, playing with Tarot cards rather than being an adult and calling him again. Playing games. I'm going to finish these cards and my drink, have another cigarette, then I'm going straight over there.

Card 7 represents how the situation influences the questioner at this time. Love card. *A new awareness of romantic love.* What if he's not even getting his messages? He could have lost his phone. I know plenty of people who have lost their phones. Could be he doesn't even know I've called.

Card 8 represents how others view the questioner in this situation. Transformation card. *The need to let something end.* What "others?" Does everyone else know? Maybe everyone knows and is laughing at me.

Card 9 represents guiding advice for the questioner. Four of Cups, upside down. Which means: *acceptance of the situation.*

Yeah, right, like I'd take guiding advice from a deck of cards. As if it's even clear that there is any "situation" to accept. Where's my ashtray? I need another drink.

Card 10 *represents possible outcome if things continue on the course now taken.* Card: The Fool.

Oh my God, I am a fool. No, this is nonsense. There, one more message on his phone. Very sweet this time. He's going to call. I just need to have faith in the right things. I didn't shuffle these right anyway. Otherwise I wouldn't have so many Cups cards. I just need to give the cards a fair chance. Do them right this time. Then I'm going over there...

Shuffle fourteen times. No, twenty-eight times. One, two...

-- Carley Berg
(What's Your Sign? Anthology)

The Color of Sound in the City

Gray down on the rooftops,
pock marked and feckle.
The streets, store glass,
white automobiles.
Black heads and blemishes,
acne scabbed and oozing.
The train crossing,
pigeons on the platform,
garbage cans. Splinters,
tears, cracks and holes.
Silence is afterbirth.
Downed wires, downed trees,
a bird's nest and three spilled eggs.
Someone left breathing.

-- Michael H. Brownstein
(Poised In Flight Anthology)

Narcissus

    after *Narcissus* by Caravaggio, circa 1597-1599

Hung head, there is Narcissus.
Endlessly gazing, still and alone,
breath steady, slightly parted lips, hair swirling,
elaborately-designed clothes, viridian-patterned shoulder,
dark lake, sleeves rippling gracefully
with golden, moon-lit cheek and fingers touching water.
From truth to downcast eyes,
given beauty is shallow;
being lovely seems all.
Reflect on that

That on reflection
all seems lonely being
shallow. Is beauty given
eyes downcast to truth? From
water touching fingers and cheek moon-lit, golden with
gracefully rippling sleeves. Lake dark,
shoulder viridian-patterned, clothes designed elaborately,
swirling hair; lips parted slightly, steady breath,
Alone and still, gazing endlessly:
Narcissus is there, head hung.

                -- Candace Butler
                (In Gilded Frame Anthology)

The Kiss

    after *Der Kuss (The Kiss),* by Gustav Klimt, 1907

Your kiss is
folded under my breastbone
like a note you left behind.
When the night exhales,
I take it out to read again.
It says: *soft lips* and *wild berries.*
I say: more.
It says: *wait for the unfolding*
to begin.

                    -- Christine Clarks
                    (In Gilded Frame Anthology)

Requiem for Icarus

     after *Landscape with the Fall of Icarus*, by Pieter Bruegel, 1558

When we met under Picasso's force field eyes
I was drawn by the angle of your shoulders
and the curvature of your smile.

Out of the clear blue sky
I fell like Icarus in love
and barely heard my own drowning
when you erased me
and started a new page.

I went blind as Monet,
staring, and still wanting waterlilies.

                -- Christine Clarke
                (In Gilded Frame Anthology)

The Last Letter Ever Written

When communication was finally re-established between New Earth and its satellite worlds, explorers scavenging for usable materials discovered the last letter ever written. Entombed in a vault in a gigantic brick "postal sorting center," (we assume that was the purpose of the building), the letter survived the nuclear holocaust that obliterated Old Earth. We speculate it owes its survival to being at the center of a heap of what was then called "junk" mail. Although the heap was reduced to ashes, one solitary letter endured. Carbon dating on both paper and ink confirmed the blurred postmark, April 28th, 2059. Since Old Earth was destroyed the next day, and since no other postal centers have been found, let alone mail, this must be the last letter written on Earth.

While scientists completed their painstaking examination, satellite worlds were encouraged to hold contests to guess the contents of the letter. To make the contests more interesting, no information was given regarding the writer or intended recipient. Romantics, of course, believed it to be a love letter and agonized over the pathos of the beloved never knowing of the love. Cynics found it equally likely that the missive was what was once called a "Dear John" or "Dear Joan" letter breaking off a relationship.

Pragmatists deemed it most probable that the letter, though handwritten (that much was known), was probably a matter of business—an offer of summer employment, say, or a request for funds for a charity. Sociologists relished such a possibility for the light it would shed on customs of the past. Writing letters was such an anachronism in their society, for they communicated by thought waves, instantly transmitted and absorbed by anyone selected by the sender to receive them.

Other speculation about the letter's contents ranged from a birth announcement, an invitation to dinner, a thank you note, a query requesting information, or even a chain letter. This last puzzling item (how could paper form a chain?) required research before professors could enlighten us that a "chain" letter simply meant a communication which was to be resent to as many people as possible (a "chain of people") less something dire happen to the recipient. How that could possibly happen was left to the philosophers when they had finished answering the question of how many angels could dance on the head of a pin.

At last the scientists had finished their examination; the reading of it was simultaneously transmitted to all the satellite worlds:

"Dear Glenda,

You haven't written in such a long time that I fear for your health and safety, dearest one. (Ah, sighed the Romantics, it is a love letter.) Please don't think ill of my concern. After all, you are my youngest, and mothers always hold their last child closest to their hearts. (Not a love letter then, but such tenderness is inspiring.)

Your new job frightens me. I know that you are a brave and intelligent woman, but the idea that you and you alone have the "launch missiles" code imprinted in your brain, that you alone could launch the next world war by keying in that code is alarming. I've kept your dyscalculia a secret all these years, but I'm beginning to think that for your sake—and the world's—I should reveal it to your superiors.

If you have, in some fashion, overcome this handicap, please let me know so that I may rest easy again.

Your loving mother, Susan"

-- SuzAnne C. Cole
(Point Mass Anthology)

A Wild Gallop Across the Heavens

Through a hollow darkness the Cherokee son traveled. He looked up to see a moon riding the skies, and stars galloping across the heavens. Carrying the searching song of his soul, he journeyed on until he came to a mountain that he looked through___ to see another world beckoning him; this was the world that held the spirit of all things.

He walked through the mountain to come to a strip of sand that stretched from the boulders of his rock-solid loneness, and the turbulent waters of creation. On the sand grew the sacred tree blooming with blue and yellow blossoms.

He threw his poncho over the edge of a nearby cliff, jumped onto it, then sailed off in the skies. The winds carried him for time to come. Hours or minutes; years or days? He couldn't know. He called out to ask the sun daughter. She was flying beside him: her wings iridescent in the starlight, as she fluttered around the badger in the skies. Being in a great hurry, she didn't reply. In a whirl and gone: her wings whirring rapidly even as the Cherokee son went floating along slowly, aimlessly ___ through the naked space of immensity. First, over a river foaming with sea spirits bubbling and gurgling with new life. And in the next moments of the first moments, he was flying over the island of horned men. These, the first men, stepped out from the rocks of creation, only to be banished to a jungle island this side of tomorrow.

'I am sailing time to creation. But am I flying forward or backwards?' he wondered.

Leaning out into the night, he listened to know. He heard the heartbeat of the world. Still, he didn't know. *'Is it beating back in time or onwards?*

Now flapping sounds: the wings of a thunderbird flapped to thunder cracking. Streaks of lightening flashing all around him. He dove into a mass of clouds, then looked down to see the sun daughter taking cover amongst the leaves of a wet-green tree; little flickers of light were bursting from her sunray body.

Suddenly, the sun appeared; she was looking for her errant daughter.

The sunray daughter held her finger to her mouth; she whispered to him, *"Hush."*

But the sun was persistent. She carried a bark torch that lit up the corners of the skies, and found her daughter huddled in a leaf-lit tree. She chased her off to the skies. The sunray was sprinting around the night clouds when he waved goodbye.

Above him, the light of a bloodless moon, and the earth but a shadow of the spirit world.

Below him now, a kingdom where a doe and buck were walking across wetlands. Stands of elks were drinking the waters to prepare the flooded lands for planting.

Leaving the wetlands behind, he sailed above rock-grounds interspersed with spiny thistles. Bare-branched trees held owls that turned their necks to tell him that he was heading to the island of the girl who lived amongst wild wolves.

He believed the owls; *'aren't they the creatures of wisdom?'*

Now, howls. Below him, wolves with hollow haunches, and eyes that gleamed in the dark. A fearless girl was throwing bare bones on the earth. And from these bones sprung more wolves, and they too were howling at him until the girl shouted at them: "Hush."

Around a bend that took him to the skies above diabolical spirits with pointed teeth and seven-toed feet. *'These dark spirits cause unwary travelers to disappear into thin air.'*

He took refuge within a mass of vines draping the trees. He waited there for the sun. And here she was, rubbing open her sleepy eyes. How tired she was; being awake all night searching for her sunray daughter.

The Cherokee son rode over the waves of earliest dawn now breaking across the skies in rosy prisms: the light being reflected in glints riding the currents. This same river was running beneath the Cherokee son; then beside and beyond him___ to empty into the vast and deep sea of his journey.

And in the broken dark there appeared a light that called his name. Appearing before him, mirrors reflected within other mirrors. Looking into the mirrors to see who he was becoming, the Cherokee son saw first the faces of his six grandfathers, then his father's face: his. One unto the other, and all moving past sunrise into a settled day.

-- Susan Dale
(Point Mass Anthology)

My Homing Pigeon Heart

My homing pigeon heart: eternally it wings me
On a long journey back through time
We follow the north star to the lake
Of Neptune's song and mermaid hair
And land beside that ramshackle cottage
With a carport on the side
And the porch with the swing
Where I fell in love
The pigeon heart comes to roost
Atop the broken chimney
It tucks its wings close to its sides
And coos and doves
While I wander through the ghosts
And cobwebs of the carport
To open the back door and walk across
The kitchen's black and white tiles
I see the washing machine that sits by the stove
I hear it churning and wringing
The fabrics of time
There is a parakeet by the window, he whistles in the sun
And because it is a hopeful spring
My father is planting a garden
And my mother is so young
Her eyes sparkle and snap
My brother is playing ball
In the empty lot by the carport
And my sister digs inside her box of paper dolls
She sees that again our bunny has chewed
The dolls' skirts and arms
Then I wander outside, and hear the lake
Of Neptune's song and mermaid hair
I say to the pigeon sitting atop the chimney,
"We must go now for I have lifetimes
Of tragedies and triumphs to live."
But my pigeon heart says, "Why go?
Always we come back

For don't you remember
It was a spring of hope?
You fell in love on the porch swing
Your father planted a garden
And your mother was so young
Her eyes sparkled and snapped

     -- Susan Dale
     (Poised In Flight Anthology)

Losing Feathers

I fall back
naked and spread
white wings fold back like hotel sheets
peach velour blanket on skin
bedside lamp shines on Pizza menu
and corkscrew borrowed from the front desk
secrets wet the borrowed bed
voices in my ear
I turn neck into shoulder
but I know right from wrong
that it's silly to sleep with someone
I can never love
especially when each time
I trip and fall
on his hardness
impale myself blissfully
someone else is feeling the shaft
a blade in the back
tossing sleepless from nightmares of truth
I may comfort him
think him dumb
but he is sharp enough to sniff out my lies.
There is nothing virgin about my wings
they are tainted and tattered
as a gutter pigeon's
I peck and I peck
at the last bit of flesh
bewildered by the strength of my own desire.
It's a burn every time
I return
as much as I would like not
to hold the weight of his heart
it's gigantic throbbing pulp
I am flattened by it
can only snake out an arm
from beneath

text an SOS
plan another meeting of bodies
even knowing
blood will shed.

-- Cassandra Dallett
(Poised In Flight Anthology)

This Boardwalk Life

(Bruce Springsteen, 4th of July, Asbury Park)

The storm heads dead on
for the Jersey shore
Of course she does
She is named Sandy
If you don't
know the words
you should not be here

-- Jessica de Koninck
(Of Sun and Sand Anthology)

Without Thread, Here, We Are Connected to Everything

These are good questions to bring to the undertow,
the shadowy silt that can muscle us deeper into the tide,
past where the tide becomes manageable, past where
the steam of the ocean peters out on the sand in a near
ecstatic teasing. These are good questions we ask the dry
sand as it becomes wet sand, holds its breath under water
for long portions of the day. These are good questions
to whisper into the reeds, where the small children's arms
become too tired to bring their large shells up the wooden
stairs to the vacation home or the vacation motel across
the street from stucco condominiums. These are good
questions to ask while refusing to look at the moon, the draw
of the scene, the curtain and the pulleys of it, and as we
concentrate mostly on the passing of time, we have other,
more important questions about our own bodies, about
the wonderful feeling of being dirty in water and never
knowing what part will remain with you underneath the low
flow of a beach shower. These are good questions, the small
queries we have about our own imprint, shrank to actual size
next to the tremendous sea, about our relevance and lack
of hold on the rope that rolls the entirety of what has brought
us here in the first place. We have questions, many questions,
and with such a context laid out in front of us, we have no choice
but to believe it matters most of all that we ask them out loud.
These are good questions, the empty shells, cracking underneath
our toes are simply a beautiful distractions from the pressure
of the sun, which has seamlessly taken the place of the moon.

-- Darren C. Demaree
(Of Sun and Sand Anthology)

Hatteras Evacuation

Today's breath felt tropical, morning rising,
a taste of something foreign in the wind's
accent.
         Bands prowl like animals, slink across
a clear blue sky. The light shimmers and sparks,
shifts and fades. Side by side, fear trails,
                      centrifugal.
We wait for the litany's next name to be called.
I will remember to trail my left hand against
the walls of every new maze. The sand knows
the fear of being lost
                far away from home.
It hunkers down, for all the good it does.

        ***

In the daily offerings of abandoned periwinkle
shells, seaglass and driftwood, the summer
slows to a stop. Labor Day restless,
the broomsedge nods to us.
              At home, a comet-track
scratched on a weatherman's cave wall
flickers on the snowy television. No prophet,
no prophecies.
            The sea's belly barely rises
while it holds its breath, and the searocket aches into
blooms fuller than yesterday.
              *Beauty is the mouth
of the labyrinth*, Simone Weil said, *and at the center
is God waiting to eat us up.*
            Or if not us, our house,
our sand, God tucked in a storm big enough
to dissolve all Hatteras back to creation's
                second day.

        ***

Anticipation carries the worst weight, heavier
than sandbags at 2am,
                       squeezes us tighter
than the Tetris of dog crates, suitcases,

a child's carseat.
             Beyond the crepe myrtle,
our neighbors toil in their separate bolgia.
Like inmates, they bob and dive, dive
and bob.
        As if Dante made them hammer
boards across windows for all eternity.

               ***

            We wander in order to stay.
                    The line of cars
            our own dust-and-ice comet tail across the
            sound.

That's all any of us can do, our backs watching
                 the tangled locks of some heretic, whose
                 name
                 we whisper like a curse, as she emerges
                 from the horizon.
                 The sunlight will shift
by the time we're across the sound,
falsely hail us with sharp-slanted rays, mocking
some Renaissance Annunciation.

               ***

The palms have begun to hail our cowed
exeunt omnes.
             Heron fled inland before us,
dusk-colored paracletes, their coarse croaks
mock of our own warbled displacement.
                             Cowed,

no one reaches for the hems of fleeing saints
who seek quiet retreat from crowds.
                                         We're waiting
for a sign that no prophet will arrive in town
this week. No temple veil shall be rent.

-- Andrea Janelle Dickens
(Of Sun and Sand Anthology)

Metamorphosis

with apologies to Franz Kafka

In the morning, Seymour, the pachyderm
awoke to find in his own *Metamorphosis*
that he had grown feathers and tiny wings,
an aquiline beak and three-toed claws in place of bulbous feet;
and so astonished was he and so ashamed
that he locked himself inside his room, vowing never to leave,
to make certain that no one else could see
what had become of him or hear him cluck
instead of rumble and roar; and there he stayed with little to eat
and little else to do than loll in the mud all day
while pondering his fate as his weight once great
became less and less and his body more sleek
and aerodynamically appropriate for flight
until, at last, after several attempts at suicide
by rope, gas, and bird seed laced with arsenic
it occurred to him that he could fly away
become a warbler or a jay or the parakeet
he longed to be in a tropical paradise by the sea;
and so he stood on his window sill, clucked *"bon voyage,
cruel world of my miserable past"*
and leaped into the air, too late to realize that the bird
he had become was a chicken (not even a duck) unable to fly—
farewell, Seymour, goodbye, kerplunk!

-- Neil Ellman
(Poised In Flight Anthology)

Staying Put

    after *A Woman in the Sun*, by Edward Hopper, 1961

He paints me naked in an empty room.
Like I need nothing. Like he needs me.
I'm his type.
High tits. Lean shadow,
blond hair falling
past my shoulders.
A long drink of water.

There is no escape.
But the window to my left is a promise.
Wide open. Green hills.
"Hold still!" he says.

So I stare at the painting on the wall.
Another landscape, this one contained
by a white mat, black frame;
it, too, allows for dreaming. But it only
goes so far, then hits the wall. Like him.
Only so far before he drops off-grid and
disappears into the canvas. No
wonder I can't stay still.

The room holds little. A bed, my shoes
abandoned underneath. A pack of
cigarettes. My restless heart. A rectangular shaft
of light pours in from an open, second window and
the breeze plays with my hair.
"Fix it!" he says.

I tuck the wisp of hair behind my right ear,
just the way he likes it, then put my hand
back where it belongs.

He says his favorite thing is painting sunlight
on the side of a house.
"So why paint me?" I ask.
"So you'll stay put."

-- Alexis Rhone Fancher
(In Gilded Frame Anthology)

Sun and Sand . . . 'Flip Side'

And the stitches on your foot will be coming out when?
No, dear. High tide is NOT a police matter.
Yes, that fence belongs to snobs. Not to elites, like us.
No, don't touch that shriveled thing. It caused you.
Don't take mom's 'piña colada'. It comes with a free cabana boy.
Mom's spf 999 didn't work. The high-end dermatologist is next.
No, those gulls didn't steal dad's checkbook. Read the above.
That is not a bird's egg. Rather a mother allig . . . OMG! RUN!

-- Elysabeth Faslund
(Of Sun and Sand Anthology)

Before

we removed our strapless dresses
from bedroom closets
satin skirts tissue paper puffed
glass vanities covered by
cosmetic compacts
slid into gardenia bubble baths
that scented our homes
like Amazon jungles
this was the time in our lives
we danced
fox trot mambo meringue
hips swaying
arms entwined
before JFK Cuba Dr. King
the Berlin Wall
dog days
before college started
and we waited with our parents
until the last minute
before the doorbell rang
for our dates
crew cut boys
who wore three button suits
narrow ties
talked about nothing
but power money muscle cars
too us to eat
at beach clubs
where we inhaled menthol cigarettes
through Audrey Hepburn holders
drank Singapore Slings Brandy Alexanders
Whiskey Sours
and afterward
beside low lit pools
on sun lounge slats
we explored each other's bodies

as the untouched moon
glazed the blue-back Atlantic
German U-Boats grazed
only sixteen years before

> *-- Joan Fishbein*
> *(Of Sun and Sand Anthology)*

SandSurfing

*"The sea stimulates words, and on
good days it seems its celebration
was made for us . . . "*

-- from "The Sea," Gabriel Mistral

Eyes closed, you and the sandpiper know
the peace where mind becomes ear,
thought becomes the roar of waves.

>The sea knows the shape of our music
>in the long curve of an oboe of driftwood
>waiting for a breath deep enough to stir it.

The sea knows durable styrofoam hearts
and plastic bottle top stomachs.
The frailty of human currency
in its broken sand dollars.

>The sea knows morning dew
>on tall spring grass through the sparkle
>of seafoam, in damp curves left
>on the beach when the tide pulls back,

the stripes of endangered tigers
and thriving zebras that race in herds
along the grassland – through its worn shells.

>The sea knows the colors of the desert –
>rattlesnake tan, bleached-boned white,
>and autumn sunset purple,

the texture of desert wind on rock –
smooth sandstone and pockmarked lava,
barkless wood and wave pitted glass.

The sea knows the brevity of a monarch
butterfly's life by the fast moving shadows
of red-tailed hawks on the spirals
of heat off coastal hills.

    The sea knows we carry the weight
    of the world on our backs and time wears
    it sea glass smooth, until we drop
    our burden, let it shatter on a bluff.

The sea knows the evanescence
of our souls – seafoam bubbles left
behind on water-stained sand.

        The sea knows our hunger for God
        with the persistence of sand.
        It knows how to reflect the sky.

        -- Trina Gaynon
        (Of Sun and Sand Anthology)

Prologue: Alternate Version

"Help me.
 My name is Zelda.
 I am in the castle dungeon."

No,
he thought, instead
fervently shaking
a fairy
he'd caught in
an empty jar.

Her voice,
and the one in his head,
a constant
droning,
boring into
what was left
of his
boomerang-addled
brain.

Thinking to himself,
go ahead and rot,
maybe you should have named
the legend
after me.

> *-- Jessica Gleason*
> *([Insert Coin Here] Anthology)*

Choose Unwisely

It was a forgotten basement in a forgotten building in the middle (geographically) of a bankrupt city, where I found her. I was taking photos of the neglect and she was crumpled up against a wall.

They were my best shots that day.

Tossed over a collection of boxes – edges torn or rotted away – she was sort of folded over her own knees, blonde hair flipped up and hanging down to her ankles.

I have to admit, for a moment, I thought she was real. I thought she was dead and my day of relaxed photo taken had just been given up in favor of explaining to the police why I was trespassing in this part of town.

The lack of stench should have been a clue, but I had no idea until I got close enough to feel for a pulse. Even then it wasn't the dust, as thick on her as on the windows, that caught me. It was the coin slot on her spine.

It was disturbing how her cold silicon skin moved under my fingers.

I was a photographer though. With no death to report, to mourn, there were photos. Sprawled in the dust across the boxes, she was realistic enough to make some striking images. I worked angles to make the pictures more desolate than lurid.

Even in cities not bankrupt, I'd yet to see such a lifelike bot. Could someone build this degree of realism in their basement? I should have left it at that. Don't disturb the ruins, was the whole point of this series -- to show the sadness of life gone by, of a world changed and abandoned -- but I couldn't let go.

It was the coin slot.

Cash had given way to cards. Cards have given way to credit fobs. Long before the city crumbled, everything had gone digital. I couldn't remember coins being common.

I had one though; in my camera bag. It worked as a screwdriver, a miniature lever, or a size reference. I knew it was there. And now I had a coin slot.

I couldn't help myself.

At worst, I'd have to replace my coin, I thought. That wasn't the end of the world.

When she sat up, I nearly bounced off the ceiling.

"You have... five minutes," she said in a slightly mechanical tone. Her mouth moved, but not quite with the words. "Insert coins for additional time. Please identify players."

She stood drawing my attention to her nudity. Her designer had given her a generous figure; if only he'd included clothing.

"Please identify players," she repeated.

"Only me." I said it while looking for an input switch, but she was surprisingly advanced.

"One player. Please choose level."

"Easy." I didn't need to think about that. I did not want to find out what she could do the hard way.

"One player, easy," she repeated, blandly. Mechanically. "Please choose game."

"What games?" I glanced behind her for a rulebook, like I would have overlooked it while photographing her. Maybe in one of the boxes she'd been lying on?

"One player, easy," she repeated again. "Game one."

"Not game one; what games?" I flipped the lid of the closest box, hoping for a manual. What I got were strap-ons and handcuffs. Body lotions in a dozen different flavors. All covered in a

decade's worth of dust. I grimaced and jumped away. If that was game one, I hoped there was an off switch. Or she was more passive than I was coming to believe.

When I looked back at her, she was turning away from the third box. She wore a fedora and carried a tommy gun. She missed some important details, I thought, as the gun grazed a naked breast.

"See, Copper," she drawled as she backed away, "It wasn't me."

A bullet zinged past my ear and chipped the concrete behind me. I was too scared to do anything but drop to the floor.

"I'm innocent. I'm not going down for that murder, see. You'll never catch me alive!"

The last line was shouted over her shoulder as she ran, the tat-tat-tat of the tommy gun echoing through the massive stone structure. I covered my head with my arms and waited for the noise to stop, watched a bullet spin on the concrete floor two feet away from my face. I was afraid to follow, and afraid not to.

How likely was it she'd find a real person to kill in this deserted city in the few minutes she had left?

How sad was it that I was already planning to hunt down more coins to play again?

-- Marilou Goodwin
([Insert Coin Here] Anthology)

Christmas Dawn

Spot of sunlight on the glazed river
    like grace.
Now no children in the house
gives it a different tone.
A rule not to look into
the mirror after sixty-five.
Man on a porch with
either cell phone or cigar
an exhausted Santa.
Wild Persian cat sinuous
through the withered garden.
On the horizon a church spire
    like a sail.

-- Ray Greenblatt
(Conversation with a Christmas Bulb Anthology)

Poem to the Asshole Blasting Angry Birds on His iPad

please disregard and don't confuse
my thoughtful stares directed your way
because in my head i'm really thinking
of slingshot-ing you across this bus
and out its open doors
watching as you and your iPad
splatter like a starfish, bloody and flesh full
on the coal-black bricks of the apple savings bank
just across this rainy and oil drenched street.

-- John Grochalski
([Insert Coin Here] Anthology)

Portraits of the Unseen

after *Chasing Mirrors: Portraist of the Unseen,* by Anilah Azaden, 2010, at The National Portrait Gallery London, UK, Somali and Afghan youth translate their names

a slate
an electric storm
who arrived recently
walked from Kabul to Tehran
is feeling her way across a new skin
who sang to me quietly
in the corner unseen
wants to teach
silvery grey

*-- Marilyn Hammick
(In Gilded Frame Anthology)*

Astrobiography

I have this friend in science
who tells me how he learned
astrophysics. It goes something
like this: You first lean so closely into
the source of things that
distant stars, whole galaxies,
collapse as if into the eye
of a great storm called God.
And what is important then
is how long you can hold your own
eye open to the center of mystery –
which is your lens –
as if you'd just discovered
some incomprehensible
petroglyph in a dark cave
somewhere under France maybe
only you have no light
but your own imagination
and the ocean called language.
Then as if the universe itself
were lethal oxygen
you breathe wonder in
    slowly

at the speed of lightheadedness.

-- Ed Higgins
(Point Mass Anthology)

Echoes of the Game

I lay back on the examining table
head turned sideways toward the monitor,
a cold spot of gel
and then the press of the medical joystick
against my neck.

Another video game I do not know how to play.

I am hoping the object of the game is to
create tangerine explosions in the soft gray canal,
followed by the rhythm of some alien, pulsing sea.

I turn my head to the other side.
In addition to playing dumb,
I now play blind.
No bells or whistles cue me,
only the occasional roar of my innergalactic ocean.

Now I must lie on my left side
As the joystick explores my chest
And probes beneath my breast like a bad first date.
Am I winning if there is a firestorm of purple, orange and
white
inside the cone?
Am I winning if a row of yellow ducks appears,
who turn into bluebirds against a purple sky
where stars glow red?

The nurse says by Friday
I'll know if I won.

>   *-- Liz Hufford*
>   *([Insert Coin Here] Anthology)*

Jammed Transmissions

In quadrants omnipotent
Where the peaceful blackness
Has awakened at last
In jettisoned star systems
Where in unknown eons
Now long fled
Backwards planets
Whose unfocused thoughts
Creaking with antiquity
In the ancient bones
Of that frigid void of space
Here I have lived long
Orbiting in a distant galaxy all my own
Through nightlong eons
Of falter and fail
A life form now turned to dust
In a long ago now all gone to rust
Astride a memory machine steed
Who reeks with the aroma of decay
As he gallops through
This once unbelievable and sentient city
Leaving no footprints in the lime green rain.

-- Ken L. Jones
(Point Mass Anthology)

Green Sky at Night

1.

The rain is falling
hard and straight down
each rivulet
an individual message
I cannot decode.

I wander around the house:
living room, dining room, sun porch,
kitchen, bedroom, bath
looking at the screens
of open windows
watching for the inevitable intrusion
of pooling water on wood
wet fabric on furniture

I am waiting for the after math
of a destruction
I am complicit
in creating
by not closing the windows
now: before the microscopic
mold spores begin clinging,
colonizing, covering every surface

2.

I am global warming
all by myself, melting
imperceptively where
I should have polar ice-caps
growing perma-frost over
potable spring-fed pools

This is what I look like
after the hurricane blows through
the tornado touches down
the trade winds reverse direction

There is too much to care for
on my small planet
and that I alone care
for it, dry it off
fight the invasive decay
choose what to salvage
exhausts my jetties.

3.

I am a rock
in a rock
on a rock
and the weather drips
on all three of us
wearing down edges
until my sharpness exists
in a hollow cavity
dangerously lined with crystals
deeply hidden inside like
a geode

even I am not sure
what is growing in there
what color it is
how it was formed
over the years
into something
semi-precious.

-- Judith Katz
(Of Sun and Sand Anthology)

Einstein at the Beach, 1945

Poised on a rock, his back towards the harbor, Einstein
in shorts and a polo shirt relaxes for the photographer.

My, what shapely legs he has and those sandals: open-toed
with a strap around his instep, a slight heel. Legs crossed,

he could be Lauren Bacall summoning Bogie for another cigarette.
He is grinning. Surely he doesn't know yet about Hiroshima and Nagasaki

only what it's like to be revered and to rue his one great mistake.
I think of him every time I watch the strangely prescient *Fantasia*:

the Sorcerer's Apprentice attempting his Master's tricks:
homely buckets of water turned into a tsunami. Even if Einstein

could contain his theories, tie them up like a packet of letters
shoved to the topmost shelf in the laboratory, he couldn't.

With scientists, that's not how it works: ideas shared, enhanced,
qualified, amended, and once out there made more beautiful.

The beauty of his math, his equations, cast a spell on the rest of us
so we think Einstein a metaphor for genius. He grins at the photographer,

enjoying himself this fine day, the war close to its end, relaxing with friends.
Who can blame him? Who knows what burdens his mind bears,

what private hell makes his heart ache.

-- Claire Keyes
(Of Sun and Sand Anthology)

Solzhenitsyn at the Beach

Note: Alexander Solzhenitsyn, Nobel Prize Winner (1918-2008)

I saw him yesterday
balding, pot-belly, mutton chops
lantern jaw.
When he pulled his pants down
a moth flew out.
He was wearing his
swimming suit
with a red star.

I asked him about his
after life.
"I'm happy. I go swimming
twice a day."
I told him Putin invaded Georgia.
"Why Georgia, why not Florida?
That's where they are always
screwing up democracy!"

The last time I saw him
he was doing the Australian crawl
out beyond the ropes
having a smoke
practicing his dolphin kick
leaving the buoys behind
training for the next Olympics.

-- Michael Magee
(Of Sun and Sand Anthology)

Astronaut

We are here,
side by side,
on this couch
where

I have opened and closed my mouth
a hundred times but not a single word has come out.

But
in my head I am in outer space
enjoying how peaceful it feels
to float around with little
between me and nothingness
but a sheet of glass.

-- Ally Malainenko
(Point Mass Anthology)

On the Coast

Remembrance is our religion, deep
fried turkey, bare feet slapping sand, South
African wine, gardenias, the forever
you see when you look past the shrimp boats.

Some of us aren't looking for yesterday, knowing
we all hug one nucleus. Some of us don't stop
searching for reasons—a holiday, a birthday, cancer.
Some of us can say just because, know we don't
speak of the years before buffers and therapy, let go
of monsters we can't name, while some of us pretend them away
with accusations. Some of us are an island of envy, vow
weekly phone calls, and some of us blame others
when we can't connect. Some of us notice

the houses on the beach get larger. Some of us take out loans,
max out credit cards. Some of us feel hurt when we don't
know about layoffs. Some of us wonder why we didn't
ask, or whether we disappoint. Some of us save
all year. Some of us watch us get drunk, become too lax
around the children. Some of us feel vindicated.
Some of us are rubber bands pulled
too tight. Some of us hardly need
an excuse.

Some of us don't want it
to be over. Some of us are counting
the minutes. Some of us will bring
a puzzle. Some of us will talk
incessantly. Some of us will go
for a jog. Some of us will find less
taxing ways to hide. Some of us have
special needs; some call it indulgence.

Some of us will smile through the cutting
remarks on liberalism. Some of us will angrily
defend the war(s). Some of us will
change the subject. Some of us will steal
away for a cigarette. Some of us will smell
the evidence; some of us will forget
by morning. Some of us make promises
before we even arrive—just a glass
with dinner; some swear we'll quit
tomorrow. Some of us will reflect
on the fact that no one's missing (yet).

Some will wonder if anyone enjoys these things.
Some of us will wonder why we married
into a family like this. Some of our spouses won't
come. Some of us will wonder why.
Some of us will ruminate on our own
secret problems. Some of us will stay behind
to clean up; some will hurry off.
Some of us will drive away,
hoping we do this again
soon. Some of us will drive away.

-- Jacqueline Markowski
(Of Sun and Sand Anthology)

Intelligent Design

Yesterday I learned of centrioles, tiny tubes,
within our cells that hold
together parts of our DNA. No one can quantify
what exists inside those tubes
but there must be something—
very little of our bodies are wasted
space. We are chock-full of practicalities.
Scientists think maybe
these tubes hold consciousness.
If this is true, cells release it
when we die. Like dandelion fuzz, floats
up out of cells, bodies, flies
away from us, into space—
back where it came from, star stuff.
I find comfort in the thought
that upon those same wings goes
the pain of trauma during abuse. Our cells
expel the burden, beyond
the boundaries of known physics, give
the gift of temporary flight.

-- Jacqueline Markowski
(Poised in Flight Anthology)

Arctic Flurries

                                          Spinning for hours
                                        silver needles make
                                        tapestries on rooftops.

Each
windowpane
becomes
a miniature
museum
of fine lines.

                                      O beautiful blizzard
                                      millions of icicles
                                      spilling!

Snapped open
by frost
wide awake
we find morning
laced with
snowflakes.

                          -- Joan McNerney
                          (Conversation with a Christmas Bulb Anthology)

The Properties of Rock

This holiday season
I am hoping to acquire
the properties of rock.

I could really use
a stocking, maybe two,
full of porosity.

If Santa Claus can only deliver
something so-not-*Vogue*
this year, I'll dress up
as a creature of interstices.

I wish to celebrate your simple gift
of permeability, long to weep
right through my own soft stone.

And what I want for Christmas, honey,
is chemistry. I want to be the limestone
worked on by water for eons.

And, should you throw in
three or four more books
on Great Basin paleogeology,
I'll be perfectly calcareous.
I'll be the propertied rock of love.

-- Karla Linn Merrifield
(Conversation with a Christmas Bulb Anthology)

Rosamund the Fair

    after *Fair Rosamund*, Dante Gabriel Rossetti, 1861

I could hear him sneezing before he reached me.

"Hay fever," he explained, ducking his head.

"That's it?" I said. "You came to tell me that?" Being stuck in a maze alone all day made me testy.

"No," he said, his nose red from blowing, "You're in danger. She knows where you are."

"And the king sent you to warn me? He's the one who put me here. What's he going to do, write another stupid story with a happy-ever-after ending? Right now, I need a schemer, not a dreamer."

Sneezy's eyes began to water. "The queen," he said, "aims to kill you by poison or knife; the choice is yours."

"How obliging." I smiled. "What choice shall I offer her?"

"You?" Sneezy said. "Rosamund the Fair, the king's secret mistress, who spends her time sleeping on a flowery bed at the end of a maze waiting for His Majesty to appear? What could you do?" He trumpeted into his handkerchief.

"I may have one lover, but many friends. Bring them here."

That night, the Twelve Dancing Princesses opened the meeting with a complaint. "We leave our beds to come dancing and instead of princes, we have to spend it with you," they huffed.

"It's an emergency, ladies," the frog croaked. "There has been a death threat on Rosamund."

Everyone had ideas. "Bread crumbs," offered Hansel and Gretel.

"Then when she's lost," said Briar Rose, "the queen could prick her finger on the needle of a spinning wheel and leave us alone for a hundred years."

"No," said Grumpy, "too complicated. "Have her kiss the frog and turn into one."

Goldilocks, fluffing a pillow of baby's breath before lying down next to Sleepy, said, "Spike her cereal."

Stress always made me hungry. I looked around for a snack. No blueberries left, thanks to the bears.

The prince held up a glass slipper. "Why not use magic to make all her shoes too small? Bunions can really limit the mobility of nobility," he said, smirking.

The dancing princesses nodded their heads emphatically and began to talk all at once about the time their shoes got mixed up.

"I know, I know," squealed one of the three little pigs. "We could build a tower and hide her in it."

"You could make it out of hay," said Rumpelstiltskin. "We have plenty of that around."

"No, you twit," said the wolf, "I'll just blow it down."

"But then you could eat her," the forest witch suggested, "if he doesn't yell first," she said, pointing to the shepherd boy with her candy cane.

While they argued, I picked up an apple left over from dinner and almost took a bite. Then I caught the wicked stepmother watching me. "Do you still have that recipe to die for?" I asked her. She cackled.

"You know," said the princess holding a pea, "I often notice what others miss. I think if you kill the queen, you'll still be second best."

"Explain."

"You know where he is when he's not with you? He's at his desk, fussing with characters and plot twists. He loves writing more than you or her. Do you want to settle for that?"

A day later in the castle, the queen threw open the door to the king's chamber. He looked up from his writing and frowned. "You know how I hate to be interrupted," he said. "I'm almost done."

She plopped into a chair and plucked a red apple from her pocket. "You missed lunch," she said, smiling. "Here's food for thought. Maybe it'll help you finish."

He took a bite. "Couldn't hurt," he said. Then he keeled over.

I entered the room as soon as I heard his body drop. The queen picked up his story. "It's about us," she said in surprise, handing it to me.

"But what a shame," I said. "It lacks an ending. May I?"

"Be my guest," she said.

I dipped the quill in ink and gave the story a positive spin.

"I just love happy endings," the queen said.

I smiled. "And they say women can't write."

-- Jane Miller
(In Gilded Frame Anthology)

Space

When you grow up with the moon in your back pocket
there's nothing that can pull you through the sky like that --
no kite or balloon, no memory --
everything else is a street light in trees.
It was the first fire that high in the morning of space
as we, planet bound since the first glimmer,
planet to planet reached.

Do you want to know a secret? Then look
at Mercury, Gemini, Apollo on the Cape sleeping
in dreams that pierce the shrouded heights;
and the torches struck from above
that lit the eyes of forest children
while thundering a breach that shook us
out of shorts and spears. Then, look at me
and my face will tilt with the arc of Saturn Fives
while shrinking to a small child's whose father
memorized the circuitry of "Godspeed, John Glenn"
and took him to the astronauts.

A child for whom Kennedy's dream is the only boyhood force
that remained loyal in all circumstances;
whose father is Jupiter, whose mother is Europa,
whose family flies from moon to moon like today's air traffic
and who searches for another marble world
adrift in space like the only place called home.

-- Bradley Moorewood
(Point Mass Anthology)

Incarnation

God came, incarnate, two thousand years ago
in a land oppressed by occupation soldiers;
conceived by an unwed mother;
lived in poverty,
broke religious laws and traditions
which kept people down,
and was crucified
as a criminal;
his birth, life, death all clothed in categories
of disdain and shame.

If God were incarnated today in this land,
would he – or she – be born
to a welfare mother with six children
and an incarcerated husband?
grow up in public housing?
have dark skin?

Would he be convicted of healing without a license,
of feeding the poor – like the Black Panthers did –
on the streets of the city?
Would the prosecutor assume he stole
the bread and fish?

Would he be jailed for overturning tables
of those who create Ponzi schemes,
the moneychangers who make deals
to move all the jobs out of a community,
or entice customers to purchase homes
with mortgages they can't afford,
those who redline neighborhoods,
or target advertising of lottery tickets,
cigarettes and alcohol to the poor?

Would he be assassinated
or sent to a high security prison

to stay in a small cell
twenty-three hours a day
for life – if you can call it life –
or to the electric chair?

Around here these days, God,
it's three strikes and you're out.

> *-- Wilda Morris*
> *(Conversation with a Christmas Bulb Anthology)*

The Synaesthete

    after *Improvisiation 31 (Sea Battle),* by Wassily Kadinsky, 1913

shoving your art down my throat
I choke on colors and sounds-
a Kandinskian Braille of bump-along trails
and willy-nilly symbols pockmarked
with squiggles scraping me inside out

your paintbrush tip smudges grey grout
inside the creases of my brow

reality becomes mixed with fairy tale-
a magician with slight of hand caring less
about the subject and more about the trick

waving your wand makes me disappear

I want you and I don't

as you hear me gag on your abstractions
you see indigo
seeing indigo you hear me gag

you've made me into what you think I am-

cold-
but not crack-the-musical-whip kind of cold
more of a cowardly egg yolk yellow cold
losing my centered sense of self

I'm not all that I'm cracked up to be

I've learned this from *you* and for that
I ask you to beg for my forgiveness

you say-

I can't be sorry for what I paint
when the color of butter sounds like middle C
on a brassy trumpet
and bare boned black-black-black
taps out our end

your painting was once propped on its side
before it had dried
you fell to your knees deeply weeping
touched by the colored signs and musical lines
you never intended

the best comes from what we never intended-

revelations tangled in vibrations of color
sensations angles theories principles

it's always about what we never intended

you
were
released

Kandinsky

turn me on
turn me round on my side
plunge into my pigment
that was never intended to drip
purple in b major between my ribs

find something in me you've never found before

> *-- Loretta Oleck*
> *(In Gilded Frame Anthology)*

On Display

Looking upward from the bottom
of a smooth-walled white-walled pit
he wonders:
Could it possibly get any colder than this?
Could the early morning air
tear more savagely at my nostrils?

Poke me hard in the eyeballs
and see if it makes any difference
stars still visible in the sky at this hour –
couldn't one of those lights
be a slowly orbiting spaceship?

Come down, dive down and remove
me from this inhospitable waste –
take me, shave me, study me, display me
as a curious cultural artifact
neuter me, generalize me
as a typical representative of my species.

In your ultra-modern exotic menagerie
awed visitors will gawk and whisper: see
how he counts his digits
over and over, sad pathological behavior –
never guessing how happy I am
that I still have digits to count.

-- Jeffrey Park
(Point Mass Anthology)

Quiet Edges

    after *Quiet Edges*, by Elizabeth Catanese, 2012

You wake up in the winter night
in a room the size of everything,
and walk the house that presses on your shoulders.
You are in over your head
in space, line and point. You wonder
how to count, begin calculations, weighing breasts, thighs,
resume, publications. Here is a place to put your body,
its past history, its hollows smelling of shame,
its stomach grumbling, empty, fat.
In Euclid's time there was no clear distinction
between physical and geometrical space.
You struggle with angles, elements,
a game of Twister with yourself,
a game of Operation, properties of space,
theory of perspective,
questions of shape, size,
relative position of figures --
to measure yourself.
Does the body fit expectations? Does it fit
the soul? Your arm is too short to span
the terrible length of Solstice night.
A shape – the Sun – at a far distance
answers. *Then I will open my hand*
and raise the light.

                      -- Faith Paulsen
                      (In Gilded Frame Anthology)

Pisces horoscope
Stay indoors, avoid tuna
Mercury rising

> *-- Andrew Periale*
> *(What's Your Sign? Anthology)*

Aspects (haiku sequence)

a cradle for life,
the odyssey never ends;
alien eyes watch

ground control could not
comprehend the vastness of
agoraphobia

blue box falling through
Time and Space; adventure waits
for the Traveller

-- Freya Pickard
(Point Mass Anthology)

White Vessel with Inverted Triangle

After White Vessel With Inverted Triangle, Ceramic, Gordon Baldwin, 1989

God's man bird –
Stricken in the scrubbed light.
Starved of the air
   that played with his feathers
     like the jibes of children.
White on white in snow bleach.

Hug your smashed wings
and listen through the ice
To the earth song
To a whale's mewl
To the snowblind rush of wind
To Powderface;
the councilor of fallen whispers.
To the dying jabber w*rds
as the last sn*wflake melts upon your tongue.

-- Winston Plowes
(Poised in Flight Anthology)

Red

for sabrina macias, on lock-down

a caution shade of combustion all appetite:
Revlon red lipstick that mimics arousal &
pornographic, vermilion fingernails
accentuate a splayed erotic;

red hair kissed by flaming fire,
a sensual awakening, Ann-Margret's purr,
a perfect flint to start a quarrel, or bullet
that portends a war;

fist-tight crimson resurrected & flung
into scorching solar wind,
white phosphorous phoenix, all molten red
& gold immolation.

& frightened russet sparrows
running red-light scared
& brushfire sweep of abandon-ship crows
launch into arsonist auburn sky,

before an obsession with the pyre, terror-blind
terrific as all Creation.   ascending angel ablaze
& dancing as Divine, a red rebellious heart
burning, rising from the stake, to cardinal
conflagration,

to red-shift reincarnation
at the igneous end of panic, scarlet obsession
to vaporization,
to crematoria bone-gray ash, reborn
an unrequited, yet intimate, act of passion.

-- *henry 7. reneau, jr.*
(Poised in Flight Anthology)

I Have the Blooms

    after *Three Faces in Lush Landscape,* by Minnie Evans, 1959

and when the blooms are gone
I have the green. I see
the Spanish moss hang thick
and true as God's own beard,
through leaves that brush away
their shadows from his eyes.
He dances by my hand
with colors whispering words
into each flower's perfect,
patterned face. They bloom
and live their day within
this garden's endless pulse.
Six hundred shades of green;
I've seen the God of each.
I've seen.   The God of each
of six hundred shades of green—
this garden's endless pulse—
He lives the day within
its patterned face, and blooms
into each flower's perfect
colors, whispering words.
He dances by my hand
with shadows in his eyes.
The leaves, they brush away
the Spanish moss hung thick
and true as God's own beard.
I have the green. I'll see it
when the blooms are gone.

                    -- Kirby Snell
                    (In Gilded Frame Anthology)

Astrology

The moon is new
In the house of a blind woman
Lisa says in soft lament
Gazing at the sky tonight
There's no hiding

The bottom of the world
Is abandoned to eclipse
The Hour of Judgment
Passes into Saturn's cusp
Planets are colliding

It all means trouble
Corpses in the forest
Trucks of kerosene exploding
Riots in Cathedral Square
Bangkoks of calamity

We're in for sorrow
Equinoctial dislocation
Days of fasting
Spiders at the bottom of the cup
And general anxiety

Rasputins guide these stars
The roof is caving in
The fallout in the fans
Is one part fire
One part flood

Listen
Lisa says
It's a lousy time to make vacation plans –

On this road to Armageddon
The tollbooth is expecting blood.

> *-- Russell Streur*
> *(What's Your Sign? Anthology)*

Jawing

Yes sweetie, five sharks
At the beach we're heading to in Chatham –
> *I like 'em!*

Great Whites, huge thirty foot charmers
Ghostly shadows of the sea –
> *If a shark attacks me, I'll just punch 'im in*
> *the nose!*

That's why the harbor master closed South Beach
Sharks are voracious death dealers, see
Masterful at cutting ---
> *I'll pull on his teeth, pull 'em right out--*
> *And they'll just pop-pop*
> *Then, I'll—*
> *Punch his nose and what kind of sharks are*
> *they again?*

Their teeth are shaped by nature
Engineered by the Divine
And they have an insatiable appetite
> *I'm hungry Mom--*

They were coming in for the seals, rapid fire
One nearly swallowed a little girl yesterday
White Death --
But they also give life
By making sure only the strong survive—
> *I'll just punch 'im in the nose*
> *Give 'im a bloody nose*
> *So his shark friends'll come and eat 'im*
> *They'll think he's prey*
> *Then they'll give each OTHER bloody noses*
> *And they'll all eat each other's noses*
> *And they'll all go extinct--*

It's the circle of life, drenched and orbiting
See, sharks compete with man for domination
Of the sea, the beaches
And (are you still buckled?) they instill fear
Like humans they have no predator ----

Wait-- if sharks eat seals, and seals eat fish,
does
Man eat sharks?
And so their relationship with man
Is a curious one of hunter and hunted,
Does a woman eat 'em too?
One alternating with the other.
I like 'em!

-- *Christine Tsen*
(Of Sun and Sand Anthology)

Miro Paints The Shortness of Breath

after *Harlequin's Carnival,* by Joan Miro, 1924-25

The story is told in things discovered
under microsopic investigation
of a still-life of scattered fruit;
a pear of hesitated light,
throbless apples throbbing apples,
or a thought of something tropical
and pendulous, man and woman
with tentacled children, seahorses amok.

The source of light is an exhaust
of ribosomes,
the dance of electrons in the Krebs Circus,
a jangled harlequin on a Citric Cycle of squiggled delight.

It's caught in a breath checked in mid-sentence.
It's burst in a field of rent sod,
pulling up a loam of language yet found,
every power coming through a new particle of organic
geometry.

The vital shapes hang free of cultural lobotomy.
Wave hello. Stop breathing.
Do you see molecular configurations climbing
out of random boxes
throwing taut lines for escape?
Or chopped guitar strings recoiled
into the music
between the impossible bird
and the song?

-- Mal Westcott
(In Gilded Frame Anthology)

Dream Caused By Sleep Apnea A Second Before Opening A Pomegranate Soda

    after *Dream Caused by the Flight of a Bee Around a Pomegranate a Second Before Awakening,* by Salvador Dalí, 1944; *Birth of Venus,* by Alexandre Cabanel, 1863; *Impression, Sunrise,* by Claude Monet, 1873; and by Claude Monet's *Rouen Cathedral series,* 1892-1893

I stop breathing,
place the church key on the bottle top
and try to pry it open.
I'm anxious to be stung,
sprung gasping into the safety of consciousness.

Monet with a collection of fizzy bottled drinks,
thumb on the lip and ready to shake:
blackberry d'aubergine;
tangerine at sunrise, rippling Le Havre;
clemetine in the light of spring;
sang de cerise.

Anything can happen before the bottle opens.
Carbonated blood flows through a hole
between the chambers of the heart.
I look closely at the monitor,
the bubbles appear as pomegranate seeds.

But, Cabanel, mon dieu, never opened a bottle.
He sculpted Venus sundaes
with maraschino borne on meerschaum,
garlands of sanguine cherubs.

Dali shakes the pomegranate.
A bee drifts in, expecting a fecundity of seed,
a mass of frog eggs spilled caesarian
on earth of flat desire

heralded not by angels,
but by the ontogeny of rockfish,
tiger from tiger
and bayonet
effervescing into wakelessness.

The kidneys of heart failure sense
that the body is bleeding to death,
and act accordingly.
Cabanel's work retains fluid
until the ankles swell and breath grows short.

He hates Monet and his spritzer works.
"There is no place for sodajerks
in the Acadame de Beaux Arts."

Monet holds the bottles to the sun
at Rouen, and turns them, each day,
in a different light.

It's still dreamtime and not too late
for anything before rising,
for a fruit so red, torn open,
to become whole, or to rend further,
to disperse in a cloud of spume.

Nothing you need to do
ever happens in dreams.

The blue smoke of exhale
rises into morning.

-- Mal Westcott
(In Gilded Frame Anthology)

The Moon is a Body

The image arrives
decades late
having travelled through too much darkness
to comfort anymore

There it is
evidence of a crisp unambiguous lip
The moon becomes a body like any other
a body that ends

The dreams we've hung from the myth of night suicide into colder day
Our children begin questioning if stars too belong to the world
They grow so much older in our silence

Some argue it was better when reality remained a theory
when there were things we couldn't touch
I realize I haven't touched my own face in some time

So I toss the moon
in a shoebox of postcards
unanswered letters
watches seashells
and other proofs of my life

In time it will yellow and crack
into memory
and I'll rediscover that heavenly body
in the attic
beneath a pile of family photos
I'll dust the cobwebs
from its milky surface
and fondly remember what I once believed

-- John Sibley Williams
(Point Mass Anthology)

Picasso's Blue Paint

Based on Picasso's Blue Period, which was a reaction to his friend's suicide, 1901-1904

All things begin when they are gone.

My friend is a part of the blue night –
why did he decide to take the world;
where did he take it?

I mix red paint so hard,
it turns blue as a period on a sentence.

I make so many blues, no one can count them.

My room is a maddening ocean of remembrance
of things I do not want to remember.

Of this, I am sure –
there are more things hiding more blue than releases them –
all of them, gone; all of them, forgotten – like a woman
forgets which lover's name she cried out as indigo paint;
like a man responding to the tug of moon on his loss.

-- Martin Willitts, Jr.
(In Gilded Frame Anthology)

Reflection: After the Great Wave

Come
forget
how loss feels
like a vast door closed
on the promise of dry land
or a window overlooking tsunami
damage so severe even our precious language fails

until revenge filigrees your hair like light, like nails
tearing at your eyes and flesh as you tell me
you wish you could understand
why pale bodies rose:
children, seals,
egrets,
foam.

-- Robert Wynne
(Of Sun and Sand Anthology)

Off Key West, Hemingway Sails with Homer

This evening,
Even my life insurance doesn't reassure me of my worth.
I am left conceiving my death for my sixty-first year.
Then others will imagine how I rode the high tide of this wine-dark sea,
Singing myself now like one of the men fated to be devoured by Scylla,
An expendable sailor who had peeked ahead in the poem and so knew his fate.

I confess to the sea and the gulls and the sun,
How tired I am of all this dreaming,
Of plunging a knife in our captain's back and throwing his body overboard
Just to say I could.
But I know I'll never awaken from this poem.

And every rosy-fingered dawn,
The master still walks the deck, shouting orders, encouraging our hearts.
My only comfort is my knowledge of Scylla,
Which no one believes,
Especially my comrades who are destined to join me.
They ask me why I seem so sober,
Now that the swells are taking us home;
They laugh and tease me that I just miss the killing.
That's right, I tell them.
A good cry would make me feel better,
Especially if it's not my own.

-- Ron Yazinski
(Of Sun and Sand Anthology)

Research and Development

Let me first say that the last thing
Our company ever considered
Was the creation of a video game
Based on the concept of Christmas.
But since your First Church of Birmingham
Was willing to finance the research and development of it
As a way to teach your children
The fundamentals of your faith,
We were willing to attempt it.
Rest assured, we chose only our brightest
To initialize this project.

Not surprisingly,
Though several of our staff graduated MIT,
And others Cal Poly,
They knew little of the Nativity story.
After I related the bare narrative,
As best I myself could remember,
I confess they were less than enthusiastic.

As Project Manager, I admit my best days are behind me.
When I suggested an interactive Holy Family angle,
In which players can change the parameters of the story,
By making Joseph something like a mason instead of a carpenter,
Or giving Mary several other children;
Or setting the whole thing someplace else in springtime,
My ideas were dismissed as passé and derivative.
But my staff knew I was just trying to jumpstart the brainstorming.

"There's no killing. What are we supposed to work with?"

"Well, there is the slaughter of the Holy Innocents," I said.

With that, there was a pixel of hope,
And that's all that is so often needed.

Brendan, our star, the brains behind
"Rock and Roll Roulette,"
In which every drug overdose could be your last,
Said, "Forget the Peace on Earth angle.
"Suppose the star that those Wise Men were following
"Was actually a Terrorist Angel
"On his way to blow up hell,
"When his charge prematurely ignites,
"Creating an Aurora Borealis effect."
We all liked the visuals that suggested.

"Yes," interjected Omar,
"And because the angel never tells them
"To go find that stable-thing,
"The shepherds have to fight off wolves,
"Hundreds of ravenous wolves,
"That should have been eating their sheep."

Gaspar, who never initiates a discussion,
But always adds insight and sophistication, said,
"Then we can show the Slaughter of the Innocents
"From Herod's soldiers' point of view.
"A simple beheading is worth five points,
"A complete disemboweling ten,
"And the piercing of twins with one stroke,
"A full twenty-five points."

"But the player is penalized fifty-points
"If the Jesus kid makes it to Egypt," said Nasim,
Adding the spice of jeopardy
That all the best selling games have.

Brendan added, "What if the babies were somehow
"Booby-trapped by their mothers,
"As a way of retaliation?"

Statements like that are the reason
Brendan is so widely admired in our industry.

This tact may be more violent than your congregation
Is comfortable with.
But I speak for our entire organization
In saying we have a winner on our hands.
Kids today are used to this level of casual mayhem,
And their parents will, for once, be pleased
That their children are learning
One of the basic stories of Western Culture.

As always, the graphics will take the most time.
If you wish to go ahead with this project,
And speed is essential
If we hope to have our product ready
For the next holiday season,
Please send a picture of Jesus
You are comfortable with.
Everything is a go at our end.

-- Ron Yazinski
([Insert Coin Here] Anthology)

A Light of Their Own

-- for the young victims of a double-suicide, Lyon County, Minnesota, April 2011

Pale yellow butterflies,
wings like worn cloth,
aloft,
in a light
of their own,
a light made candescent
by misguided
dreams,
slights dragged
so deeply into spirit
they bruise the flesh,
small fears worried
into large, heavy knots.
They should be fluttering
above the aster and the bluestem,
lightly and unburdened.
But we find them in raftered
shadow,
swinging,
wings flattened,
light doused,
and even more pale.

Ah, why not wish
for a world gone mute?
Butterflies wounded,
dead,
and I ask for this.

-- Dana Yost
(Poised in Flight Anthology)

The Somatic Art Critic

after *Artist's Model,* by Ralph Basford, 2005

Scoliosis in the bare back of the standing nude
speaks to her from the side-lit painting,
its nude's loosely draped wrap like a curtain
torn from *Gone With the Wind*'s plantation house
not velvet red but the color of sun-struck root beer,
the gallery all but empty right before the opening.
Tell your model to get some treatment soon,
she says to the absent painter carefully absent
even from his artwork set on the wall like a window
for Peeping Toms with too much free time from jobs
lost in the late downturn that promises to leave
this painting on the wall absent a "sold" sticker
until it comes down at the end of the month.
She sees through to the model's skeletal scheme
like the exaggeratedly angular tree in the drawing
next to it – maybe outside the nude's own window –
perhaps recalling how Renaissance painters
built up their figures by layers from bone and sinew
to the draping of flesh like this nude's spare coverlet,
sculpting surfaces dictated by bones beneath
that speak tonight to this body worker seated
on the gallery's lone bench before the crowd comes in
to see and to be seen, unaware of a trained eye
that sees as the painter saw, through practiced hands.

-- Ed Zahniser
(In Gilded Frame Anthology)

From the Journals

To Cheating Ex Boyfriends

(inspired by Lucille Clifton)

I wish them endless nights of sadness and confusion,
I wish them the swirling internal pain of being cheated on,
I wish them bad headaches and loss of appetite,
I wish them a false hope of getting over it,
I wish them a weep-a-thon on a Monday and the last tissue.

Let them believe that they were right so that when they
have daughters, they will know that they were wrong.

-- Shaquana Adams
(June Napalm and Novocain)

```
5ive syllable hook
Se7en syllable image     n
Then end with a t     r
                  u
```

        -- Alek Barkats
        (November High Coupe)

sleePMapnia

woke with the highway
interstate system drawn up
and down my body

>   *-- Alek Barkats*
>   *(November High Coupe)*

The Things

Between the two of us
you'd think
we'd leave less behind
but there are baskets
in the hallway
full of phrases left in their wrapping
suppressed advice
compliments of course.
There was the time
I didn't tell you
that I loved you
and the time you didn't say
"I wish you'd die"
along with the fern and goldfish.
It doesn't matter now
in that hallway
with its
opposing doors
we each took one
and simply
walked away.

-- Jon Bennett
(July Napalm and Novocain))

3 Fish in a Pool

Walking the bike path
I stopped at Cordanesus Creek.
It emerges briefly from a storm pipe
goes into a culvert under a footbridge
then back into a dark tunnel.

Still, in the shade there
are ferns, trees, and a pool
though not more than 2 feet deep.
I went down the steep embankment
avoiding baby diapers
and decaying garbage
to peer into the cool shallow

and was astonished to see
3 fish in that pool,
and a crawdad, old and pale
missing an arm but still
a little lobster
amongst the filth and failing
of people people people.

Back on the path
an old woman was watching me.
"There's 3 fish in the pool,"
I told her, "and a crawdad!"
We both smiled
and the path seemed greener
and filled with a promise
that someday we'd find
the things that we have lost.

-- Jon Bennett
(May Jellyfish Whispers)

Weightless

There is no time left,
blessed and cursed as we are.

Not under supervision.
Nor hiding under a table because the enemy drops its bombs.

Flowers crawl towards your eyes.
The violent stupidity keeps me here.

No, I don't know who we are.
Not even as the light declines.

We walk the streets, kill mice, stand on snails-
Weightless in the great stillness.

-- Joop Bersee
(July Napalm and Novocain)

Damnation

Her hunger has no clothes.
Her shoulders offered, wreaths
the remains of a battle between
wind and wind, dull wind lying
on a stone, close to the high chair

of king and father, sweat like
pearls breathing into far fields,
a turtle o so slowly, away from child
and tree. The sky sings like a dog
shivering beneath its bony skin.

A daze of thoughts takes my arm
to a car full of remorse, just a few
words floating to the surface as
the world begins to move through
the black wooden gate of damnation.

-- Joop Bersee
(June Pyrokinection)

Smoke

When I gave you up I missed your fingers
like unfiltered cigarettes, brown as bourbon, long
as trains headed out of town. I kept seeing them move

the way some hammers move. Every day I reeled
my thoughts from the telephone, the cool receiver,
craving the short beige sounds you'd offer
before you pressed end. Air felt blank, just breathing.

I'm troubled by your music and the taste
of reverie, the hourly crackle of wild fire. Smoke
drifts west over miles of scorched sand.

-- Abra Bertman
(June Napalm and Novocain)

Me O' Clock

The day see-sawed into night
And I, standing at the edge of the fulcrum,
saw the moon rise again
into nothingness.
Cactus breath and heartbeat drops
falling into
dreary ice wallpapering the
insides of my eye.
My mind karaokes to the tune of
the waves and the winged moths
behind the bushes.
My voice peels itself to reveal the
tortured body of the shriek within.
My bare feet the daughters of
illegitimate ecstasy and misbegotten inhabitants
of the forest floor .
The blue colored tendrils from the ocean
climb up the cliff,
gift-wrap my body and soul into a
haloed hug, overpowering me.

Life is best experienced as a freefall.

-- Shinjini Bhattacharjee
(August Pyrokinection)

It is not true that
all toast lands butter side down.
Not all toast gets dropped.

> *-- Sara Bickley*
> *(November High Coupe)*

Pinched

yes   yes   yes
egg faced sand tango's
stone legged tourists smile and break
soap edged guillotines lather weary grey palings
orange peel crabs drink stinging bees—
running barefoot on the melting ice

contemplating

the sledgehammer jabbing away at my coward spirit
like lightning chewing on an albino cat:
while cars drive by worth more than my last five working
years
and i worry about losing the next.

-- Brenton Booth
(February The Mind[less] Muse)

Silence in the Woods

Brother Joseph sat quietly on a fallen log listening to the sound of the brook. He raised his bamboo flute to his lips, took a breath and set himself to blow. Just then he heard a violent snapping of twigs, and a boy, perhaps ten years old, came crashing out of the brush. He spied Brother Joseph and, veering from his course, ran up to him crying, "Help. Help me." He collapsed at Brother Joseph's feet, gasping for breath, "Man broke into house. Got my folks at gunpoint. Says he's gonna kill 'em. I got away. Need help."

"Did you call 911?"

"Got a phone?"

"No. Up at the abbey. Come with me. I'll show you the way." Brother Joseph set down his flute, picked up his crutches, climbed to his feet, hobbled slowly up the trail.

"Can't you go any faster?" cried the boy.

"You go on ahead. It's just a hundred yards up this trail. Take the right hand fork. Big wooden building."

The boy said nothing, just dashed away, quickly disappearing from sight. Brother Joseph took a few more steps, then stopped. *He'll be in good hands now,* he thought. *Nothing more I can do.* He returned to his log. Sat down. Picked up his flute. His heart was pounding hard. He listened to the song of the brook as it coursed over the stones. He brought the flute to his lips. Someone was coming up the path with slow measured steps. A bolt of fear shot through Brother Joseph when he thought it might be the gunman. His friend, the postman, emerged into the clearing with a sack of mail.

"Hi ho, Brother Joseph," he called. "A beautiful fine day it is to be carrying a sack full of bills to the abbey. Here is your Smithsonian Magazine."

"Oh, look at this," said Brother Joseph, taking the magazine. "What is this strange bird on the cover? It's a hoatzin, whatever that is." He opened the magazine, searching for the cover article. His eyes fell on a photograph of a gigantic robot arm, so delicate, said the caption, that it could juggle three eggs without breaking them. Quickly he closed the magazine. "Please, my friend, take this up to the abbey. I'll look at it later."

"Busy?" asked the postman.

"Busy trying to quiet my busy mind. Why, just now ... never mind. I'll tell you later."

"I see how it is with you, my friend. I'll be on my way."

After the postman left, Brother Joseph tried to settle down, but he kept thinking about the boy. *What was happening up at the abbey? What about the boy's parents? An armed psychopath less than a mile away. Why hadn't he gone to a neighbor for help? Probably one of those lone houses at the edge of the woods. The woods would be safest. Good instinct to run for cover in the woods. A robot juggling eggs. What for? Who would want to?*

He couldn't silence the voices in his head. Then he realized that by trying to calm himself enough to play his flute he was doing it backward. The trick, he knew from long experience, was just to play the flute until the babbling voices stopped. He raised the flute to his lips and blew a note. A long wavering note that came from his busy mind, then a quick string of notes, still connected to his thoughts. As he played he again became aware of the brook singing among the stones and he answered the watery song with his own song, the notes now coming from deep within him, flowing harmoniously with the stream. He was focused now. The world narrowed to the water music mingling with the fluty wind music, no room for thoughts, no other being but here now.

Once more silence in the woods, except for the song of a bamboo flute, a running brook, a distant gunshot.

-- Bob Brill
(July Pound of Flash)

A Body's Language is Sometimes Written in Latin

One morning you roll over and wake to a stranger,
your body splintering into hard time.
Suddenly fingers do not remember how to lift a fork,
feet need a rhythm to climb the stairs,
even hair refuses the demands of a comb.
At the hospital, they make a study in mistakes,
the hard gurney bending too much into the wrong shape,
doctors arriving to play doctor, tests made, blood drawn.
They check your ears, look long into your eyes,
move you from one room to another, tell you to go home.
Sometimes there is nothing more anyone can do.
They send you away with prescriptions for pain and swelling,
directions you can barely see, your eyes so full of fire,
the skin surrounding them sulfur yellow and rotting eggs.
So it goes. All of your life this is your body.
It did its work and brought comfort to you.
Tonight you try to walk a straight line down the hallway.
Even in bright light, shadows are instruments of pain.

-- Michael H. Brownstein
(January Napalm and Novocain)

A Chain of Days

They tell me how jail cells cleanse the soul,
How hard nipples of silicon implanted breasts have a quality of egg yolk,
The sky a burden of sweat and peroxide,
How window casements shake with a current in rain.
I am a lonely old man who cannot remember the past—
Yet I know the honey locust has thorns sharp enough to break skin
And fruit from the persimmon tree will stop an eye from twitching.
How much of anything is true enough?
I raise my hands high over my head and bend back my neck.
Muscles pull at my calves and force my feet to their toes.
Punishment is always harder on the one punishing,
The crime between her legs is silk and rose blossoms and the soft fabric of terrycloth.
They explain the way an accident can happen and how something done on purpose
        can be an accident, too.
Rain washes away stains, bad breath, easy smells sweet as sweet oil easing the
        tension of mucous caught in the ear.
They tell me how the autistic distinguish darkness from danger, how the whole
        distinguish a blemish from a scar.
When morning comes, they will tell me more secrets.
They will allow the rain to continue to fall.
Some of them will not be able to look me in the eyes.
I can tell them how silicon implants are like rocks behind felt.
I can tell them how missiles are made of flesh
I might even explain the motion necessary to break through the initial skin between
        legs.
Rain holds magic. Alone, it offers me a chance to sleep.

                        -- Michael H. Brownstein
                        (April Pyrokinection)

Slice of Utopia

the end of days dance
in your head as your
only child buries your
feet in the white sands
of a tropical beach

this slice of utopia is
your personal hell

a nightmare you never
envisioned or cared to
think would ever exist

you can't help but think
this is some form of
slavery and you can't
understand where the
happiness comes from

ill-equipped and never
prepared the demons
understand what must
be done

your son laughs as the
water rushes over his
feet

tears stream from the
corner of your eyes

when does a nightmare
ever have a happy ending

-- J.J. Campbell
(July Pyrokinection)

The Mermaids Won't Tell

The mermaids won't tell
of the myriad dreams drifting out to sea
that you burnished with soft youth,
then abandoned once caustic questions posed
by grey-haired mere-men of dry bones, petrified ears
and glass houses filled your head.

Nightingales in oak trees won't retrieve
the secrets stuffed in knots on hot
summer nights, chock full of adventure,
blisters and sweet laughter, open to the constellations
granting all creatures the right of passage
when they listen, heed full passion.

Gnashing bears won't stop, stalk past you today,
'though in old guise they sniffed, relished
your air, stroked hard-packed earth where
bare feet hammered before diving
among ghee pools, faces slathered in voracious skies
marling innocence and carnal desire.

I would give you my broken basket filled with icons,
a reliquary of love pilgrims who never lost their aim,
but the maze you desire hobbles, blinds you --
you'll never reach the center
to find your way
out.

-- Theresa A. Cancro
(December Pyrokinection)

Leaves

between blue sky, blade grass
spaces, I sense a shift up and down
my anchored essence, the fall

of autumn night draws me,
prunes easy strides in sandals
even as it streams red, gold,

amber, they drizzle on the sides
of grifting breezes, excoriate notions,
left over pyres of love in the backseat.

-- Theresa A. Cancro
(November Jellyfish Whispers)

Seething Blue

The turquoise of the Mediterranean
never clings to me.
It smiles, disappears
as I plunge hands in
like I plumbed your depths
but saw no reflection there.

Malocchio* watches now,
unblinking on the side,
as I grip weathered oars.
Uneasy calm, a brusk wave
tosses my open heart,

buffets fishing boats --
black lies stare.

-- Theresa A. Cancro
(November Napalm and Novocain)

*The evil eye

Peace

It all comes down to choosing.
Choosing to swim through my thoughts,
we silk around my ankles dragging me down,
or to sink.
Breathe out worthless air
and drown in the calmest of waters.

-- Valentina Cano
(May Pyrokinection)

A Wedding Gift to Remember

Wind gusted off the ocean, sandpapering the weathered sides of the beach house and rattling the wood shutters. Outside, a chair blew over with a bang. November's storms had arrived. Summer on the cape was delightful, but fall weather was iffy.

Ellie took a sip of non-alcoholic wine, grimaced, and turned on a lamp by the couch. Her parents had been wonderful about the pregnancy. They were always just a telephone call and a hug away.

The chick-lit novel she'd been reading didn't hold her attention. Ellie shoved the book aside but not before removing the envelope serving as a bookmark. She took out the embossed invitation inside and read it again: *Sen. and Mrs. John L. Fley and Mr. and Mrs. Mark F. Jones request the honor of your presence at the marriage of their children Cindy Ann Fley and Richard Malcolm Jones...*

She didn't bother to read about the wedding ceremony or the reception at the country club. They were over and done, like her brief affair with the groom.

Richard had breezed into his sales manager's job at the auto dealership with a smile, a ready laugh, and the confidence that comes of graduating from Dartmouth and going to work at a business owned by his father. He cast his eyes about the office and stopped with Ellie, slim and blonde. Soon they were inseparable, attending summer stock productions, dining at seafood restaurants, and enjoying art house movies.

"This is wonderful," he said one moonlit evening, "but I want more time with you alone." He gazed into her eyes as they walked barefoot on the beach, savoring the salty air. Waves lapped softly at the shoreline, and tendrils of foam collapsed and vanished into the sand.

"My parents have a beach house," she said, mischievously. "We could be alone there."

He paused. "Really?"

Ellie sighed and looked about the room, cluttered with seashells, polished glass and other treasures from beachcombing. It had been a weekend to remember.

And then Richard met Shannon. She was everything Ellie wasn't: the graduate of a prestigious women's college, a lawyer, and the daughter of a U.S. senator.

Richard dumped her. Ellie was shocked by his betrayal and his reaction to the news she was pregnant.

"Whose baby is it?" he demanded.

"Why yours of course," she said, taken aback. "We can get a paternity test if…

"Forget it." He licked his lips. "I can get some money if you…"

"No," she said. "No!"

He turned away. "Then it would be better if we didn't see each other any more."

That got easier the next day when she was fired.

The wedding invitation came as a surprise. She hadn't gone, of course. But she decided to send a wedding gift. What could she give Richard and his bride that would stand out among the other gifts? Ellie took another sip of tart wine, grimacing again. Boy, could she use a glass of real chardonnay. After thinking about an appropriate wedding present, she settled finally on glassware. But not just any glassware.

The newlyweds would be back from their honeymoon in the Bahamas now, ready to open presents. Hers would be a surprise. She could imagine Richard's bride saying, "Well, here's a weird gift from one of your old girlfriends. She sent an ordinary water glass. Why, there are even fingerprints on it."

Ellie smiled. They'd have a laugh at her and then notice the two pieces of paper under the glass. They'd read them. And then the laughing would stop.

The glass had come from a luncheon meeting at the auto agency on her last day of work. When everyone had left the room, Ellie had picked up a water glass where Richard had been sitting. The first piece of paper was a lab report detailing what the glass revealed — his DNA. The second was a note:

Hi, Dick. You can look forward to being a dad as soon as the baby is born and I find out its DNA and match it with yours. Better get ready to break out your checkbook!

Love (not), Ellie.

-- Arthur Carey
(July Pound of Flash)

Not Enough*

Pluto –
    153 hours in a day,
Moon –
    656 hours in a day,
Mercury –
    1416 hours in a day,
Venus –
    5832 hours in a day,
Earth –
    not enough.

-- Fern G.Z. Carr
(July Pyrokinection)

*Hours are equivalent to the time it takes the planet to make one rotation on its axis.

Glucose

~~keys::locks::doors~~
swinging
o[pen]
closed

                      stuck

unhinged
in some haphazard fashion like the

smile _{hanging} from her
dis[illusion]ed lips the NIGHT

she walked away – that NIGHT
I said "p[each]es" when I
should have said "apple"

~~fruit~~
low-hanging fruit d[angling]
from a *dead*

     tree
in some concrete grove filtering the lives of
barren women
and *fetid* men;

men like [badge]rs chucking and fucking and

pret[end]ing to love her
dis[illusion]ed lips holding
up the haphazardly hinged smile like
some rotten fruit oft [romantic]ized by
grizzled faces

   at   l a n g u i d   paces
in some coffee shop on the edge of town:

"apple"
she s[cream]s

and on my own tongue I still
taste

p[each].

> *-- J.R. Carson*
> *(February The Mind[less] Muse)*

Warm

Drunk cuz o'sunshine,
see that clover?
Pick it and tell 'im
he's pretty.
Men like to be told
they're pretty
too.

-- Joseph James Cawein
(October Pyrokinection)

Drizzle

I carry a knife
When I find the right person
Fingers fall like rain

-- Martin Cohen
(February High Coupe)

MRI scheduled -
red maple's crown riddled
with blossoming clots

-- Corey Cook
(June High Coupe)

Leafing Out

Hillside smolders –
smoky green wisps unfurling
as sun burns through haze.

-- Corey Cook
(June High Coupe)

The Frenzy of the Red Berry

They appear en masse like some outlaw biker gang
descending like locusts, raining like toads, pelting the earth
like children spilling into the playground, drunk and tumbling pie-eyed into the 2 a.m.
dawn, racing full throttle around the yard, swooping then flashing
in rust colored autumnal solidarity
Swoosh swoosh, they dive, their wings beat frantic like all existence hinged on it

Beating one another out as if embroiled in multidimensional chess
without deliberation, like huns chasing down the Sabine Women, screaming, shrieking
Aerial dynamos, daredevils, hot-dogging hotshots, rebels without a pause
Engaged in some cosmic carte blanche ribbon cutting all-you-can-eat heat

Orbs of red clusters, vulnerable as testicles, bright like lanterns
beacons of temptation, picking them off in their yellow beaks
gorging greedily, ripping at 'em like Promethean entrails, stealing and
resting their feathered corpulence on bobbing branches, hearts rapid-fire, pitter-patter
swallowing as they seize another and another, more and more

They are everywhere in a flash—20, 30. . .
hurtling and Hitchcockian, spinning, twirling like spastic lariats
dashing dipsomaniacal, magically avoiding collision
without yielding one feather of cartwheeling cocksurety

Four robins, i imagine to be the senior sages
splash, giddy and gaga in the concrete birdbath
the anchor of this hub
Wiser perhaps, fatter it seems, more mature, possibly, they vie for perspective
like old men with little hard-ons they cheer the youngsters on
splash and wade with uncontained zeal. The flurry of
berrymania, berrypalooza, berryphillia, filled with an insatiable gluttonous crimson fed
narcotic-fused, feather-stuffed, birdbracing ecstasy
these seniors shake their heads, pump their birdy fists, catch their reflective colors
splash with glee and rejuvenating joy, dip, flap, flutter, lowering their
bright plump bellies, displacing the brackish water, shake the wet from their wings
before rejoining the youngsters
Join or Die, and maybe join then die
in between which—fly fly. . .

And then it is over
as instantaneously as it began, as if some secret alarm had sounded

and they take to the greater elsewhere, the big blue, beating passage
returning the scene back to the calm that prevails
as the yard settles
beneath the yellowing maple and its stripped bare branches
its nearly fallen leaves, spinning twirling seeds, concluding
with bunches of untapped berry clusters
left behind like random booty from an interrupted robbery

The air reverberates with their departed energy
like a battlefield after the fact only no where near as sad
as a big sleepy orange tabby crawls out from under somewhere

This brave voyeur saunters out, watchful cautious, travels the seed
laden lawn, the crab grass, moss, clover, twigs, scattered berry husks
shell-shocked worms, nervous beetles. . .
leaps up upon the birdbath, sniffs the tainted water
does not drink
gazes philosophically into the sky
blinks
then continues on, disappearing slowly
into the dying azaleas and fallen foxglove

-- Larry Crist
(March Jellyfish Whispers)

Theme and Variations

"The rain drizzled its effects over the whole scene."
(from a letter)

Your lips drizzled their effects all over my lips.
The President drizzles his effects all over the nation.
Mothers drizzle their effects over their children.
The lie drizzled its effects over the marriage.

Fortuna drizzles her effects upon her favorites.
Money drizzles its effects over love
when love isn't drizzling its effects over money.
History drizzles its effects over the present.

The present drizzles its effects over memory.
The billy club drizzled its effects on the marcher's head.
The priest drizzled his effects on the congregation.
The moon drizzles its effects over your naked breasts.

Language drizzles its effects over everything.
Beginnings drizzle their effects over endings.

-- Philip Dacey
(January Pyrokinection)

Passions *(a haiku string)*

Body sacrificed
Mind a'tremble
In a service of the heart

    *****

Without a fear of vertigo
Down the dizzy path of infatuation
I slide

    *****

The volcanic heat
Of being
Imbued with you

    *****

Your letter arrived
A heady fragrance of words.
Clinging to the pages

    *****

Irrevocably forever
Smoky hot
Inwards

> *-- Susan Dale*
> *(January High Coupe)*

The Funny Thing Is

I thought about hugging you this morning
how your stocky body fills my arms
and that maybe if I squeezed hard
you'd be
ok.

Just ok
just not broken anymore
an aching abandoned boy
bones shifting around unhappily
under all that muscle
all that sunshine I used to call your skin
it does light a room
but maybe that was hunger
illuminating your man shell
wiser women would have run
but I wanted to touch it
feel the warmth of your pliable insides
all those guts your mother twisted up
mixing your batter till your idealism and revulsion for woman
was all syrupy like regurgitated Robotussin
burning on the way out
but sweet I mean Damn!
most of us are ridiculous enough to enjoy adoration
we just never understand the price of it
I was your pop star dirtying my reluctant pedestal
you sticking cameras in my face
tripping me up with questions
and broadcasting my failures all over the place
I didn't want to be part of it
your slippery image
one minute your "good girl"
the next minute "a loose woman"
I see now how you were turned to an object
a babysitter masturbating on you
a mother who threw you away

I get it how
you need to fuck on top
so as not to suffocate
I do too
for the same crushed down reasons.

-- Cassandra Dallett
(February Napalm and Novocain)

Found a Pawn Slip

for the diamond
I bought you.
How much more fun
it was
on the way up,
then this extended
fall.

Drove past you just now
on the street
recognizing
piece by piece
the clothes I'd given you
black Pea coat
black Jordan's
black hat
too late
with a flash of reddish brown cheek
my horn was slow
the pavement slick.
And me
pen moving blindly across a notebook
in my lap.

Now I'm texting while driving
feed I need to say
look
it's not *all*
your fault
I'm the loser
that picked *you* out.
Who's cooking dinner,
and picking up the kids?
Did you find an apartment?

At a red light
I notice graffiti
it says "follow your"
with the symbol of heart
"Shiiiit, that's how I got lost!"

-- Cassandra Dallett
(February Napalm and Novocain)

Hyacinths in the Gutter:

late afternoons, i cross the culvert-
they are all over the 2' width of stagnant black,
huddling close, closer, one
over the other-

catch my eyes, i blink and
for a moment everything is forgotten-
the spiced tamarind puchka-mix,
tinnitus of trivial chatter-

skins of purple silk,
unfolding sugar labia outwards,
reincarnated peacocks-
origami memories float down

sip with shivering lips
green dew off leaves that conceal,
behind veined cheeks
blackness, the grim called reality

and i'd rather choose a lie,
trapped in a moment of internal stasis
i cannot feel my heart.
suddenly it is all different, like

melancholy mirrored on glass,
translations, graded violet/indigo
rubbed over with golden dust-
the skies are pregnant with inopportune rain.

-- Mohana Das
(March Jellyfish Whispers)

Discovery

The day metamorphoses
by molecule, particle, atom
one collating with the other
in what we might
understand as pixels
and the more there are
the more expensive.
So I'll look
out my window
a little longer,
I'm feeling
like a millionaire.

> -- *William Davies, Jr.*
> *(March Jellyfish Whispers)*

Spring Contest

The tree extends
its bony hand
offering ruby buds
seemingly for the taking
as if no amount
of small print
could obscure
this truth

> *-- William Davies, Jr.*
> *(May Jellyfish Whispers)*

Blink

Some leaves fall
so dreamily,
they beg for witness
as if, look,
a diversion,
something magical
if only for a moment,
the time it takes
to land on the ground
and be damned
with the others.

-- William Davies, Jr.
(November Jellyfish Whispers)

Temperance

He dipped his brush in crimson oil to paint an empty pail.
How can you tell from this angle? Turn on the light, she said.
A bucket? Yes. *And is that a dog?* Yes. It's a dog.
*There's flaw in your stroke, it's convincing, it makes me want
to tube a newspaper, strike her haunch.* Careful, he said,
headlines are decidedly harder these days. They laughed,
he fingered the canal between her knuckle and wrist,
she smiled, turned back to the canvas and touched it.
Strokes dried to points like colored teeth. I've got one, he said.
What's the difference between wind through a pail,
and thread through the eye of a button?
She sipped a plastic cup of wine, trying to decipher chardonnay
from pinot, shrugged (if it's not from a box, it's probably fine).
A vehicle, she said, *a co-operative attachment, while the other is free
to focus its attention on lack of contents.* His mind was fuzzy
from linseed oil and sauvignon. She smiled, grabbed him
by the collar, pushed him back into the couch and knelt.

Years later, they have fallen out of touch.
She calls him on a Sunday as it rains.
*How could you paint an empty pail? It's not possible
to paint emptiness, to capture absence. You'd have to be mad
to spend your life on such things.* Baby, he whispers –
he can tell she is crying, he imagines the cord
wrapped around her finger, and she, in a distant city
would be wearing a summer dress, Roman sandals
laced up her calf, sunglasses pinned in her hair –
I won't upset you, neither would I hope to paint what's not there.
I'm trying to call attention to the hole in the bucket.
You don't need to see the puddle to understand.

A dog scratches at the door. He stretches to turn the handle,
clutching the receiver between his shoulder and chin.
Is that Maggie? Yes. *How is she?* Fine, just fine.
He'd given up drinking the year before, set a ringed mug
of coffee on the countertop. The dog attacked its water dish.

I guess I never thought of it that way, painting the hole, that is.
Believe me, he said, I understand, but that's how it has to be –
what else can we hope for, if not what is, or isn't?

The dog sat watching him fiddle with the cord, smiled,
tilted its head, then shook its dripping jowls on the floor.

-- Jim Davis
(March Pyrokinection)

Emily as a Lake, a Lilac

Maybe you thought, the shore
of beauty was somehow less
beautiful? Eager to be shoulder

& splash, Emily is the lake
& the purple lilac, she is beauty
& almost beauty, she is what

shakes the walls of all beauty
& collects its to rattle heat
down from the jealous, sky gods.

-- Darren C. Demaree
(March Pyrokinection)

Adoration #90

for the manager at the Kroger's

Yes, I saw, in fact I read it
out-loud to my daughter that we
we're not supposed to ride inside

the cart, but with my son sitting
under buckle, we had no choice,
but to chance that she might, at some

point, stand up to reach for pancake
mix. The running and singing was
my fault. We were having such fun.

-- Darren C. Demaree
(October Pyrokinection)

Pick-Up Haiku

you on a diet?
'cause you're not the only one
watching your figure

give some pity sex?
some say I look best wearing
nothing but a frown

hey babe, I could kill
everyone in this room to
be alone with you

-- Jacob Dodson
(July High Coupe)

the sunset
knows I've been staring
she blushes

> *-- Jacob Dodson*
> *(August High Coupe)*

Film Noir

Lightning strikes and an old oak splits in two.
Mother stops ironing; hovers above a badly
wrinkled landscape. Dad bangs in the door bringing
with him the sweet smell of gardenias.
Crosses the den in three long steps.
Picks up the screaming phone that is tethered
to the wall with a spiral cord. Caroline,
with her ebony hair and Snow White face, is dead.
Extracted from a pile of twisted metal and broken glass;
she survived for two short December days.
A Christmas Eve funeral. Ice encapsulates
every rose falling from her casket.
That night and for the next 29 years,
she speaks to me in dreams. Always sitting in a green-painted,
wooden chair. The room, plain and dark, she turns to me:
Her face becomes a movie reel, shows details of a life I didn't know
all that well: tent camping on white-sand beaches in France, dancing ballet
with grace and fluidity, a tender first time making love, and a rape
last year on the Country Club's freshly mowed lawn.
She turns to me and plays for me a Christmas
Special: *"Things Worse Than Death"*
The hot, naked paunch of a filthy man
suspended over you. The sweat from
his hair falling in your eyes, his
fluid tacky, pooling on your stomach
and inside your ripped underwear,
the cool, slick edge of a sharp knife
meeting the thin skin at your neck so that you
swallow all screams.

-- Janet Doggett
(January Pyrokinection)

Trial Separation

"Separation" sounds scientific, perhaps surgical
like conjoined twins leaving an O.R. on separate
gurneys; one thing ends, then two continue on
or parts of a space launch coming apart, one going
on, while the other, as expected, drops easily away.
"Trial" seems too tentative, like trial and error or
better, a test drive around a block or two to try
things out, like taking off the training wheels and
watching the children ride away from us, watch
them grow away from us, trying out their new
found separateness, or like a trial-size that comes
in the mail, but then grows larger, even family size
or like something with a thirty day guarantee and
if we aren't satisfied we can send it back for a full
refund, minus postage and all this damn handling.

-- J.K. Durick
(April Napalm and Novocain)

Playing at It

It isn't a game after all, a lob just over the net
To his or her non-existent backhand, fifteen-love.

It isn't a game after all, horses at the old hoop,
Jump shots, set shots, hooks till someone misses.

It isn't a game after all, ten pins down the alley,
Strikes and spares, in the gutter and over the line.

It isn't a game after all, with pawns and rooks
Protecting the queen and the king's last move.

It isn't a game after all, just one live bullet in six,
A spin, then to the temple, then pull the trigger,

And after all that, it wasn't a game after all.

-- J.K. Durick
(May Napalm and Novocain)

Dog

She lives in this moment, like any other,
noting every shade of meaning in my tone
and gestures, reads me seriously, a book
she knows well, dog-eared, grimy, almost
biblical, the first of the things she consults
mornings and nights. She has seen me in
my weakest moments and easily forgave me,
has seen my best and easily forgave me. She
quietly watches for hints about what's next,
peeks around corners like a spy, follows me
like a stalker, shows a patience so job-like,
so dog-like that I've spent hours trying to
imitate the immediacy of it, her endurance,
how being so perfectly in the moment can last
so long, can stretch out just like she does on
the floor right here, while I write poems, poems
she is always the first to hear.

-- J.K. Durick
(June Jellyfish Whispers)

Soldier Leaves

Golden lights play on leaves,
transforms them to soldiers,

their burnished buttons glow
as they fasten their jackets

and close in beating hearts.
They mount their horses

while sulphur musts the air,
hooves pound tales to stone.

Little boys soft in mothers' arms,
snuggle into shawls as flashes

blue their eyes with dreams,
their fingers curl fragrances,

their toes wriggle with life.
Solid ground grips their feet,

chilly air reds their faces,
marches them to canon's clasp.

Buttons glow harsh forms,
steel chills peaceful hold,

lurks in sun's lull on leaves.

-- Ann Egan
(July Jellyfish Whispers)

Elephants Remember

Elephants remember
when they were small
amphibians evolving, plodding
to land on ponderous legs
how they grew and grew
developing tusks and trunks
thick skin and attitude
marching across a continent
all their own
without a predator
to challenge their size
but they now gather
around a stagnant watering hole
after a century, waiting to die,
nostalgic for their ivory days
wishing that they had evolved
to fly away on pterodactyl wings.

-- Neil Ellman
(February Jellyfish Whispers)

Fish

    after *Fish,* a statue by Constantin Brancusi, 1930

In the far-fetchedness of my life
as if a fish
I swim in violet-colored seas
and green the canyons
with my breath.
  Nothing has substance here
nor birds have wings
the rivers flow from mouth to source
and I return to the place
where I was spawned
  someday to crawl from river to land
upon on my knees through time
and mud-dark shores
to that place of prophecy
where a fish becomes a man
and man remains a fish
and I must swim upstream until I die.

-- Neil Ellman
(November Jellyfish Whispers)

The Distance You Can Traverse in a Minute

Gary woke to snow. He was fine with snow, but he was hoping for fire.

"It just goes to show, the weathermen never get it right," he said, stretching and shaking off the piles that had collected in the folds of his body.

He dressed in shorts, scanned the room for a shirt.

"Of course not."

He opened the front door. The void looked dense this morning. He closed the door and walked into the kitchen. He learned a long time ago not to open the fridge or the oven. He sat down and thumped a finger against the table.

"What to do... what to do..."

Yesterday, he walked back and forth from the front wall to the back wall for 1,440 minutes. The day before, he had walked in circles around the kitchen table.

Movement always helped. He knew what would happen if he sat at the kitchen table for 1,440 minutes. He would start counting seconds or the strands of hair on his head. He already knew he had 5,000 strands (God had not been good to him in the hair department).

Gary stood up and walked back to the front door. He opened it and looked around. He was tempted to step outside. What would be there? Who would be there? He closed the door again.

What if there was no one out there?

What if even the weathermen couldn't be found?

He listened for their voices. The chattering broke through the void around him.

"50 percent chance we'll have 20 to 1,000 meteorites hit our houses today . . . The void is about 50% denser than it was yesterday... the snow isn't really snow... it's tons and tons of dandruff...."

He looked down at his shirt and touched a white fleck. It melted on his finger.

"Oh, the boys are getting crazier..."

He sat back and let the void re-enter his head.

He smiled, remembering his wife. It's too bad he cheated on her. She really did love him. He debated again whether she was somewhere in the void. Would God had forgiven her for suffocating him? He shrugged. Did it matter?

He gnawed on his finger, pulled at the wedding ring. Nope, melded to the skin.

He went back to the door, opened it, looked at the void.

He was done with counting minutes. The minutes of a day were always the same.

He was done listening to the weathermen. They were idiots.

He was done walking in circles, sitting down, or waking up covered in cockroaches.

He was done thinking about why the books always said there would be fire. He'd never even seen a candle.

Hell, he was done with it all.

Gary stepped outside and closed the door behind him. He counted less than a minute before the void began to change.

-- Kristina England
(February Pound of Flash)

Split Ends

Jennifer knew by the glint of the knife that he was ready for her.

She lowered her body and scooted under the car. She needed time to think.

She couldn't run. He was a professional runner and her asthma would take her down in less than a mile.

Jennifer bit her lip as she watched her boyfriend's feet emerge from the weeds.

They were supposed to be enjoying a nice picnic. Champagne. Strawberries. The cooing of Spring birds. A glimpse into the mating rituals of animals. Maybe they'd even get a little frisky themselves. Okay, probably not. He believed in that whole waiting before marriage thing.

But when you date a man with a split personality (willingly), you should probably stay in public settings for dinner.

At the moment, Jacob wasn't Jacob. He was Ben.

Now if Ben hadn't been jealous of Jacob, she'd be fine. But who wasn't jealous of Jacob. He was good looking, athletic, and incredibly kind.

Earlier, Jacob had pulled over and provided his umbrella to an old lady making her way down Park.

"Oh, no, I'll be fine," the old lady insisted.

"Now, now. It's supposed to pour the whole State of Texas on our town. And you know the reputation of Texas."

The old lady smiled and took the umbrella. Then she shuffled on her way.

"I didn't know it was supposed to rain?" Jennifer said as Jacob hopped back in the car.

"Oh, it's not, but imagine if it did. That poor lady!"

Ben, on the other hand, would have shouted out the window, "Get on with it. We haven't all day. The pedestrian walk isn't for half dead grandmothers!"

Ben paced back and forth in the road.

"I'm not going to kill you, Jennifer. I just think it's time to give you a haircut."

Jennifer's eyes narrowed. Jacob loved her long hair. What would he think if she let that whack job give her a crooked cut.

"Oh darling, I'll be gentle."

Jennifer sighed. She crawled out from under the car.

Ben chuckled.

"I didn't know your butt could fit under there."

Jennifer wiped mud from her dress.

Ben stared at her hair and came closer with the butter knife.

Jennifer rolled her eyes.

"You'll never get anywhere with a butter knife. Here..."

She shuffled through her purse and removed a pair of scissors.

"But scissors are so predictable!" Ben said, stomping his feet.

"Okay, use the butter knife."

Ben jumped up and down eagerly.

The sun set as he began to saw away at her hair. She wondered how long it would take to get even a handful of hair removed.

"Do you mind if I read?"

"No, go ahead dear."

Jennifer didn't actually have a book. She looked up at the sky and watched it peel back the layers of night. When the final glimmers of red began to dissolve, she frowned.

"I never noticed how dull a sunset is..." she said.

"I never noticed how dull a butter knife is..." said Ben, throwing the knife to the ground. "How 'bout we go to a bar and drink like dirty old men?"

"Well, now you're talking! Jacob never takes me drinking."

Ben beamed as if he'd just won a spelling bee.

They got in the car and pulled away just as a Barred Owl began its mating call.

-- Kristina England
(March Pound of Flash)

How the Artist Sees the World

It's about the light.
How it slants entire worlds
With its opinion.

-- Alexis Rhone Fancer
(February High Coupe)

Haiku for My Beloved

I ask for breakfast,
Instead, he brings me flowers.
Am I still hungry?

-- Alexis Rhone Fancher
(February High Coupe)

A Quarter Past Time to Move On

Lightly torn girl of summer
calm down.
Swaying leaves float all over the sky.
A black diamond achieves brilliance.
Twilight.
Shoot the bullet that burns a hole through the heart.
You left after the locked door.
Your bright smile appears to be unclear.
Stand at the shore.
Turn around just to be given away.
He's hungry for you.
There is no substitute for starving
only waiting.
You finally gave it away for nothing.
You're not to blame
Forlorn eyes, clouded with doubt.
It's a loss to understand.
Send for the dawn.

-- Jennifer Fauci
(January Napalm and Novocain)

Un Blodymary

Hear the moaning Bedouins
In the desert night
Across the dunes
And upon the dead shrubs

See the sunlight
Spreading across the hot flat desert
Floor the shockwave flattening the rocks
And puffing the dirt in the night
The ship descending behind blue lights
And rotating orbs of bass

Sling your arm over the chair back
And lean into your forearm
Resting your head at a slight angle
On your palm

And drink your bloody mary
And close your eyes
Close your bloody eyes

-- Zachary Fechter
(February Jellyfish Whispers)

Rainmaker

Sing that song you dark rainmaker
You who stand frozen in deep stride
Over our cities of the plain
You who flash breathless whites
And snap unearthly jaws.

Sing that swirling mad twister
Of grey blues about our empty homes
You who to me are a mass of
Dreams expired in the dawn
Who's going to tie you down tonight?

Sing of that marble river
Of our chase for the mystical tiger
Of our final journey as men
And cry for us
To sweep us away

The rainmaker was a poor mummer
Just a useless beautiful map he was
But we saw the map and were
Swept away from the mindless nothing
In the reggae blue

-- Zachary Fechter
(August Jellyfish Whispers)

Perigee

You amble out,
celestial glob,
put on your pitted
smirky face,

And yet they kiss,
they laugh and touch,
they ramble on
in easy pace,

You practice more,
you snarl, bare teeth,
and wobble wide
a Western stance,

But they are loathe
to back away,
they find you still
at every chance,

They love you so,
they seek you out,
but you will not
stay dim, undaunted

You grow wild
in size and glow,
and then, aghast,
they tremble, haunted.

-- Sharon Fedor
(May Napalm and Novocain))

Memory

It's memory, they say,
the brain cap secure and work///ing
seven armadillos in momma's bottled cats[up]
the charm of a Frisco trolley.

      It's memory on the cheap,
neurons for sale
look there –
don't you see it?

      memory   memory   memory

I (re)member the tiny scampering universe
child prostitutes taking it in the rump
on Taiwanese beaches

look –
more memories…

you can catch them
if you're fast.

<<<Me, I'm lazy,
no memories for me.

>>>Laying here
in the dark
in green socks.

My brain stem
like a l-o-n-g and hungry
flower.

      -- Ryan Quinn Flanagan
      (May The Mind[less] Muse)

The Time Witch and the Forgetting Wizard

'You're mischievous' he said, putting his hand between her legs. In the corner of the Friday filled pub she laughed into his eyes and they made a date for a date. In the Friday filled pub he grinned at her keenness and sexy tights. 'Up for some fun?' she asked, rubbing against his long legs. She wanted to purr. She watched his hands. They aroused her.

Their grins were from Cheshire as they went through the orange and black night to his accommodating accommodation. 'Just a bit of fun', they told themselves. 'We can have our cake and eat it', they told themselves.

In the muddled bedroom they got naked, laughing. They had careless sex carefully. They kept their thoughts out of the room and their hands on each other. He watched his face and she smiled into his eyes. They delighted in their greed.

She saw the beginning and remembered the lopsided grin. He saw the middle and remembered the fun. They tucked away the hurt, disappointment and the betrayal under the pillow. She was a Time Witch - she could rewind time and stop it before it got to the painful end. He was a Wizard who could forget anything and everything.

But the feathers from the pillow escaped and tickled her nose and irritated her eyes. A huge sneeze blew away the pillow and the hurt and betrayal and disappointment came flying out. Time unwound to the bitter end. This was an out-of-date cake and they had no more spells to cast.

-- Sarah Flint
(January Pound of Flash)

And Tracked

Dusk settled in ,
       sirocco
               stayed away
      from shore

And the pewter
       is die-cast
              where the new
      awaits its turn
          to wax
                  again.

Steps same as earlier
      seem different,
            quick
                  on tiptoe
     through puddles
          idling at corners.

Crosswalks
     and highway dividers
are the wrinkles
             of America
        where the micro-expressions
            come to reveal
                the tells
   of bluffs made
       about upward
                       trends.

And the eye
          riding coastline
            has been
                  watching
                  following
since leaving Spain –

                          the one still standing
conquistador
given new names
          -male-female-male
                    categorized
and tracked.

                    -- Kenyatta Jean-Paul Garcia
                    (June The Mind[less]Muse)

Fading Comes Easily

Light is aloof
even with its need
to drag shadow
with it
everywhere
        it takes a moment
        to shine

How detached
luminescence
are you?

So fast as yet to be beaten

And easily shattered
with a prism
into living secrets

And taking time
each year to become
        less and less

Then of course,
fading comes
easily.

                -- Kenyatta Jean-Paul Garcia
                (June The Mind[less]Muse)

We Sorrowed Far When the Sky Tore,

but moments of union bent us
to glimpse a lavish paradise, yielding
to our bodies stripped of speech,
becoming portals to the ever-now,
our aggression was holy
as we hunted for sacred acquittal.
      Evolution, we often think of being what we are -
counsellors to elevate the potency of each other's dread.
Talk is a hood, a roughly-strewn path to our tortoise-tread.
Touch
is precision, absent of air, rattling staircases, galactic
in its suction of sand and hair and pores
that voice complaints and monetary aches,
tethered to this cruel house.
      We live inside the march, ruined by darkness.
On this earth, we have one pasture.
Churches will not do for us
what they do for others. We have outgrown
our guilt, our last names and the bitter sword.
      Our colours are common only to us, thickened
by our mischief-tar and unspoken humour. Ours is hushed
and chasing, dripping with moods, unreflected
in the polished jewellery.
      On a new planet we will be remembered,
congregating among the fractured
 as a shaft of gracious amalgamation.
      Drenched with this mercy, we will be a light switch
that spares no memory or obligation,
brightly displaying the decayed and burning,
colliding in composite, fashioned by our fusion.
      Among the first fully twined, what we are
will sprout then thrive, be immune to misinterpretation.
Dimensions we will enter as an interchange,
our feet warmed against
the soil of the moon, locking calves in place,

digging and dropping, basking
on the plains of our emancipation.

-- Allison Grayhurst
(May Pyrokinection)

Fill the Ghosts with Upward Rejoicing

so that clouds turn to fishbones
and flies become islands learning a primitive mission.
Obey the shuddering perplexity of dwarfed aspirations
and still be able to cry clear, continuing ardent,
when it is time.

I wish I was an actor, acquiring
the yolk of another's journey, or the ear of an elk
twitching at the panther's controlled inhale.

Flags and conquered greatness. Death, you
never share. You open and we watch you oil
every boundary with your vanishing act.
We smell you in the honeycomb and in the suffocating
many mutations of thriving pleasantries.
You are sharp as a broken shell -
blowing shame from our feelings,
stiffening the streets we walk on so we walk on
straight, with the purpose of a mortal silver sun.

Here and here, there is nothing, not language, not history,
only forkfuls of burnt coal and some framed pictures.
Being a traitor to survival's code, I have no use for finality.

I lived close to the rapids, skipping stones,
beating back shadflies.
I was riding my blue bike. Some almost-teenage children
hung my cat from a tree. I found him that morning,
a shadow swaying across a shadowy sky. I wasn't allowed
to take revenge or cradle him, broken, a husk, goodbye.

-- Allison Grayhurst
(May Pyrokinection)

Dead Bull's Poem

The bull is pounding sand.
What does he know?
Maybe the crowd is here for hint,
Maybe they want to see the guy
in fancy hat and silk jodhpurs
get gored through the heart,
his rib-cage battered by hoofs,
his flashy red cape
stuffed down his gullet.

But out stride the picadors,
jabbing the creature
with sharp lances,
thawing blood and pain
from his shiny brown rump.
Maybe they just want to get him worked up,
raw anger flaring through his nostrils,
muscle and bone pulsing, hammering.
They'll stand for no mistakes this time.
The matador must be destroyed.

And out struts the man in question.
The bull snorts.
He eyes the villainous showoff.
Sequins, indeed.
Roses! I'll give him roses!
The crowd cheer.
But why?
El Whatshisname is not even dead yet.

-- John Grey
(June Pyrokinection)

Study 16

The rain's shyness
Its pointillism graffiti . . .
Tattoo's impermanence

> *-- Tom Gribble*
> *(January High Coupe)*

A Poem from the Editors

Dear Ms. _____

Thank you for your story.

We aren't saying that it sucks

We are just saying that it doesn't fit with our vision.

At this time.

We know you spent hours on this story.

It's obvious that you craft your stories well.

But George didn't like the father, and we think it may be that he has

Daddy issues himself, but we won't say that,

And Rachel thought you needed more scenes

With less dialogue and more description of the

Hospital room because we just couldn't see it, you know?

When you say that the tubing hung around him like slithering snakes ready to strike

Are you implying that the juxtaposition of the snake to his head was like the birth of Christ?

Because we didn't see that.

Please send us your work again,

Please use our online submission machine

Please don't worry if you don't hear from us for a year

There're only us and two grad students here.

Yours truly,

The Editors

> *-- Judy Hall*
> *(July Pyrokinection)*

Staid, The Night

This night, the day fowl laugh hazily
Through the wafted green air-
Said night-as seeded, dazed:
And quiet, frequently-

To a realm of callous currency now:
Here fly- the frigid clipped mocking birds;
Lurching past frigid chirped contingencies-

Towards a space of tempered reality; even
Sprouts of a languid sky- infinite-
Here lie-here lies-
By lone skewered sky
Sedated, in posture- as *tripped* night.

-- Christopher Kenneth Hanson
(August Jellyfish Whispers)

A Fictional Heist

Dostoyevsky sits in sudden shock-
tumbling down the dust bound safes
and missing keys-
They are locked tight of course,
his action, known to be quite in desperation.
The crew will let sparks fly past
steel black compartments and greasy wheels of chance-
While two blundering buffoons pry and push the black kettle safe
into the mid-day light.
As now, their dear patron- Dostoyevsky now
wipes two tears from a worn cheek,
slips outside of the bank-
And remembers his father, killed by thugs-
whom used liquor to suffocate.
Stressed out completely after seeing this cogently- this image in mind,
Dostoyevsky takes his crimson bandana off- drops his paint gun rifle,
finds a space under a nearby cherry blossom- locates a ball point pen,
then finishes final chapters to *Notes From Under The Earth*.

-- Christopher Kenneth Hanson
(February The Mind[less] Muse)

A Grievance

The heart stakes out its own metaphor:
Creaky timbers shore the entrance
to a shuttered mine.

The wood sings, it moans
as the delicate balance that has held
since the last seismic shift
slips, rips cell from cell
clean down the center lines
and the structure collapses.

This was the site of the portal
to a delicate rape:
You made false time.

I waited like the mine waits
for a shaft of light
and settled for the usual:
perfumed hair, silky smooth legs
and clean white sheets
that I twist in my sleep
into a shroud for anticipation.

-- Linnea Wortham Harper
(April Napalm and Novocain)

Chilled

Chilled, you say. As in— somewhere between
five minutes in the fridge and packed in dry ice—
the right way to serve Chardonnay. *Chilled*, like
a gust of fog off the ocean slapping you hard
at the edge of truth-- no hat, no mittens. As in,
*I'm standing here wet and naked with no towel,
for Chrissake!* Or, *Keep that kidney on ice till we
land, doctor!* As in hung out, calmed down, or
frozen out of something you had hoped to warm to.
Chilled, you say, as if a personal climatological
data point could clarify as much as a good hard
swallow, or a cold crystal goblet whose wet lip
moans your song as my finger traces the rim.

*-- Linnea Wortham Harper
(April Napalm and Novocain)*

He Met Somebody at a Conference

He waited till we were in bed to spring it on me. *You **what**?!?* I sputtered. I probably sounded more upset than I was, but I had just ordered the bumper sticker he wanted, the one that says, *My Girlfriend is a Goddess from Northport,* and I was in no mood to pull it out of him piece by piece. So that's why he never answered his cell. *We didn't have sex,* he defended, like that was the point, like now I would roll over and say, *Well, cool then! What's her name? When is she coming to dinner?* Honestly, it wouldn't have mattered that much. It's a conference tradition— almost a requirement, really. The folks with an eye out find each other fast. And *bang. Bang bang bang.* But all they did was ditch meetings, take walk, and shop for clothes they had no intention of buying. They picked things out for each other, tried everything on. He just kept talking, and I held my tongue.

I was getting a pretty good picture of how it was, how she studied him, standing there with her head at a tilt while a triptych of mirrors shed light on every angle and made him a multitude. Her eyes took in the whole of him, runner's calf to GQ jowl, looking at him so intently it felt, he said, like she was looking all the way into the depths of the very black hole he feared he was, but then he would kind of flip inside-out and into a parallel universe with just the two of them. It was odd and a little eerie how it happened, and he thought that it must have felt almost like almost dying, but without the fear.

And I'm thinking what a piece of work. After confessing to three days eyeballing that tart in public, using their faux shopping trips for cover, and making it all sound like church, he wants my blessing. I always knew it was temporary, what with him barely older than my son, two little kids already, and a couple of pissed-off exes. I just didn't see it coming this soon. And last week I loaned him money. Should have known better. We met at a conference too.

-- Linnea Wortham Harper
(February Pound of Flash)

Waiting for the Storm to Pass

"What's that?" Angle said, pointing at the man's arm.

"What's what?"

"That thing on your sleeve."

The man looked at his arm, a frown on his face. "My heart. What the hell do you think it is?"

"It's beating," Angle said.

"I sure as hell hope so. Wouldn't need to worry about the tornado if it wasn't, would I."

Angle looked around the storm shelter. None of the other fifty or so occupants seemed to notice anything unusual. Most were huddled with family members, keeping an eye on the stairs leading to the exit.

He stared at the beating appendage, as it's pulse quickened, and idly raked bony fingers through his beard, not sure what to say. "What's your name?" he asked.

"Harold, but most people call me Hank." A honed edge remained on the man's voice, like he didn't want to be bothered. "What's yours? Not that it matters. I'll be continuing on my way to Kansas City once the storm passes. That's assuming the bus is still upright."

Angle thought about that, and decided the man was right—that it didn't matter. He told him his name anyway. "Angle."

"Angle?" Hank scratched his heart.

"That's my name."

"What the hell kind of name is that? You Greek or something? Shortening your name so people can say it?"

"The person who filled out my birth certificate misspelled angel. My dad was so pissed when he found out he went to a bar and drank an entire bottle of Jack Daniels."

"Can't blame him," Hank said. "I would'a been pissed, too."

Angle nodded and smiled. "I don't think I would've killed the parrot, though."

"He killed a parrot? Did the bird make some wisecrack about your name?" Hank put his fists in his pits and flapped his arms, the heart beat faster with each movement. "Polly wants an Angle. Polly wants an Angle. Waaak!" Hank laughed so hard he nearly fell off his chair.

Angle reached out to steady the old man but pulled his hand back, not wanting to touch the beating heart. "Some other drunk challenged him to a game of darts. Dad threw the first one about thirty feet right of the target into the bird's cage." A loud bang from outside the storm shelter interrupted his story. Everybody in the room jumped. A woman Angle couldn't see screamed and prayed to Jesus to save her. Just her. No one else. "The owner tried to have my dad charged with murder."

"This just keeps getting better," Hank said, as he started to cough.

Angle patted Hank on the back until the barking stopped and the heart slowed its pace.

"Hey, folks." It was a high-pitched male voice coming from across the room. "I think the storm's passed. We're going to open the door."

Angle and Hank and everyone else sat still while a large man in a Chicago Cubs t-shirt, his bloated belly uncovered, a tattoo of a hot dog in a bun with coleslaw under his belly button expanding and contracting with each breath, opened the hatch. Sunshine brightened the dim room. A breeze carried fresh air into the dank rectangle.

"Well," Hank said. "I don't know what we're going to find out there, but it was nice talking to you." Angle noticed Hank's voice had calmed to normal, so had his heartbeat.

"Same here," Angle said. "Hey, you going to get that fixed?" Angle asked, pointing at the man's heart.

"Not sure." Hank cupped it in his hand, like it was a baby's head. "It kinda fits there don't you think?"

Angle watched Hank's fingers caress the organ as they climbed the stairs. "Yea. I think it does."

-- Jim Harrington
(August Pound of Flash)

Indigo Blue Night

The sky blackened with crows
As the night dissolved bit by bit

In an indigo blue light.
My breath lay vaulted in the spring

Air as the street lights lit up blocks
Inch by inch, corner by corner.

-- Dawnell Harrison
(April Jellyfish Whispers)

Train Wreck

A squall of birds
bent down to see
the wildfire bellowing
near the train wreck
waiting to happen.
Above a blackened sky
I slept with empty dreams
as my mind crashed
against something
not called love.

-- Dawnell Harrison
(October Napalm and Novocain)

Motherless

Disappointment has another mouth
To feed in the dark asylum

Of her heart.
She reaches up to find

The sky starless and motherless.
In the silent still of the night

She reaches for innocent fingertips
And finds her hands broken and without.

-- Dawnell Harrison
(June Pyrokinection)

Color Codes

I'm like a cat looking backward
Over my shoulder at yesterday.
I see things best by movement,
Infinite shadings mixed of gray;
Black and white dichotomies
Escape the shutter of my eye.
Without the shift of real people,
Vacillations of petty purposes,
Individual meanings become lost
Among a phalanx of demands.

Sometimes in looking backwards
I can see shifting shades and shadows,
Emerald green on the edges of sadness.
I wonder why I paid so much extra as my
Color console still presents the new in
Tones of white and black and blue and red.
At least when the olden ships of state were
Granted Marque, they ran up the Jolly Roger,
You knew clearly which side they sailed for
Instead of them just pussyfooting around.

-- Rick Hartwell
(February Pyrokinection)

Sneaky

Shadows creep up on you surreptitiously and as
dawn rises to noon they trip and fall to their knees
performing silent obeisance at meridian, thinning out
towards an eastern infinity as day fades to dusk and then
into splendid sunsets: purples, reds; retinal sensuousness
dispelled by knowledge of particulate matter and vapor.

There are shades to shadows too, not just from sun, but
of moon and stars and fog; of dispersed, elusive fractals,
water beads skittering, grey fog phantoms trying to hide
in peripheral vision, trying to capture you unaware.

Moon shadows sway like the tides; adding, ebbing,
flowing through night and imagination until fleeing.
Star shadows exist, but can be seen only by night
fairies and fireflies when switched off, both keen
seers of the heavens when Selene hides her face and
stellar sylphs rule the night until her bloom's restored.

-- Rick Hartwell
(September Jellyfish Whispers)

After the Talk

Morning's first whiff, sun burnt pine,
Nostrils spiced and alert,
Better than fresh baked rolls.

Splashed water from pond fountain,
Syncopated waterfall backbeat,
Ears pricked to goldfish music.

Early breeze dislodges hair strands,
Whisked arm hairs tickle, tingle,
Water blowback chills her face.

Plucked and sucked dandelion stem,
Transports several decades,
Sweet as recalled childhood.

Mourning doves atop the ivied wall,
A third in the pine, shunned,
Sad laments from an empty bed.

*-- Rick Hartwell
(May Napalm and Novocain)*

Scraps of Paper Her Nights of Christ's Shirt

Sketches adorn many a dog eared paper
New ideas on textured napkins her open notebook
are sexy skirts of chiffon off the shoulder,
dresses silk puffy collars
and gowns of flowing designs with open backs
Stacks and stacks of drawings
Scraps of paper sketches on top of them
Drawing the evidence that her thoughts pour out
Onto pages all night insomniac gracefully
on a new sheet of 8 ½" x 11" a sketch of a
female figure with an asymmetrical sexy shirt
hands on hips long neck long legs
"printed source pg 183 Byzantium" I found
the 2" thick book on page 183 is a
Painting tempera gold leaf on wood
first half of the 14th century
from Constantinople artist unknown
the holy drama three figures
symmetrical ascendant in the
center is Christ on the cross the left is
the Virgin Mary dressed in a
blue maphorion bordered with
gold fringe and a hood standing small head
Mourning face almost horizontal to the ground
on the right is St. John the Evangelist
dressed in maroon robe over
a light blue dress flowing down covering
so you do not see his feet
holds his head in right hand sorrowfully covers his face
with blue sleeve hanging open down
in the shape of a tormented mouth
small trees popping out of the lower portion of landscape
behind the cross two small angels float above Christ's
outstretched arms held by nailed hands
a semicircle halo glows from his back to above his head

Christ is dressed in that
symmetrical skirt on the new sheet

Her journey at night traveling from the
Mediterranean to the Black Sea
on pages filled with holy trinity for a
new season of blessed garments in the
new fall collection Christ died for fashion
On the cross wearing an asymmetrical shirt
Soon to be cat walked center stage

-- Tom Hatch
(June Pyrokinection)

Tapestry

The afternoon of the new born fawn
Climbing skinny unfolded legs
Up rocky hilly pattern of weave
Wanting a leap back into the womb
Drawn possibly by Aubrey Beardsley
Umbilical cord swirls illustrated
Hoofs becoming dirty earthly
Strident with life sees the filtered light
Of the forest
The taste of mothers milk
Feeble to strength in the spring to
High summers grasses brown spotted blending
Camouflaged in the landscape of the hunting wolfs
her fear to go has turned survival stayed standing
In the dusty fibers of the tapestry my grandmother
Left me
Now on the floor next to the bed
Hearing the wolves chewing bones filled with marrow
In my to sleep every night woven from my grandmother's dreams
Wolves surrounding the frightened fawn
Still there in the morning stepping someday
Over crushed, broken, gnarled bones that
Cannot be sustained forever lying on the bedroom floor
As the fibers break down the wolves get closer to the fawn everyday

-- Tom Hatch
(April Jellyfish Whispers)

Judgment Day

Irrefutable damage,
Liaisons with Lucifer,
The deeds of the victim scrutinized.
What you bring to the table either makes or breaks it for eternity.
Dealing with the small print and all that entails.
Angels and demons hovering around ready to take you with them.
Locked in discussions over written laws and how to interpret them in this day and age.
Waiting and hoping for a bright outcome.
Regrets over what one did in that short time in that ugly little place.
Resigned to accept what will be, will be.
As quick as a flash one group grabs you and off you are whisked.

-- Damien Healy
(January The Mind[less] Muse)

Beyond CPR

No comfort.
No coalescence.
No continuance.
Experiences which can't be undone.
Words which can't be unsaid.
Feelings which can't be unabated.
No pleasantries.
No placation.
No predestination.
Wounds that are too deep to heal.
Truths that are too strong to subdue.
Lies that are too many to hide.
No response.
No recognition.
No recourse.

-- Damien Healy
(January Napalm and Novocain)

'Round Round Rodin

> *after all of Auguste Rodin's work, and the portrait of Rodin by Bordelle.*

Rodin carves curves round,
no angle, no anger, angel and human, one.
Besides the bulk of greater importance,
there is the delicate inference:
either the ether is real, or the real ethereal.
Who has he chosen to carve?
And what subject?
You and I are in his dream;
do not object to being his object.
Though cast you are not cast,
though duplicated you are not duplicated,
though modeled in a negative mold,
he models nothing negative.
Myths transcending our transgressions,
he sees all truth, but chooses which truth to tell.
When making us out of clay, he tells the truth.
When making us out of bronze, he tells the truth,
when making us out of higher thoughts,
he tells the truth if we wish to see it.
Elan Vital sculpts with élan and vitality.
Donatello donated, Rilke pilfered,
Rose posed, knowing full well the passion
he spent on her was now spent on others;
she sank in shadows of shades and young Camille,
like Despair and the Falling Man.
When you were young, you needed her rose;
when you were old, you needed your youth.
The sweet delicious art models were.
did he dally with Dalou, too?
Dante the Poet was his thinker.
My grandfather was named August, loved mortar;
but, mortified, he would exclude de nude.
How French was the Poor Mouth-ed hero of Calais,

looking the same as any other French DP
strafed or exiled by the Germans,
like so many of my French post-war neighbors.
How familiar that pose!
Incensed by your sense, essence,
Ecole des Beaux Arts: your bad, you're bad, your loss.
The boss: Auguste. That beard
by Bourdelle is bordello weird.
But in your gift, a rift: why is war a girl?
Are girls not the war inside yourself?
War is mainly man's domain.

-- Ruth Hill
(October Pyrokinection)

Narcissus

My hand stirs the water, opalescent and thinning like a fog may thin.
The mourning.
Milky eyes prepare for the shock of bright.
Cutting clear,
Tiny diamonds sparkling their worth.
They settle to a shimmer as a thrill grips me.
My reflection!
I gloat alone.
I am transparent to be carried off by the next wave.
Lulled to sleep by a stray siren's song.
Lucid only in a swift flash of memory I hope will haunt you.

-- Kevin M. Hibshman
(February Jellyfish Whispers)

Cat Goddess

Obsidian and moonstones under her pillows.
She gazes long into the clear quartz and feels the pulse beat of the earth.
She knows when you sleep and reads your dreams.
Her mind fills with pictures.

Stealthy, on silent paws, she rides the air.
Her fur stands on end as she connects with every breath alive in the night.
Emerald eyes bright and fixed on her target, her prize.
She moves to the pulse beat and danger dances wild in a world of night sounds.

She arches her back.
She winces at firelight.
Warms her fur and purrs.
The hum of the universe in motion.

Later, she dabs scent behind each ear,
Slinks into pearls.
Instinctively leaps to hide under the bed at the first peal of thunder.

Preening before a hall of mirrors.
Divining aspects of a personal mythology.
She is sleek and sure with a fierceness reserved for any true adversary.

She leaps from your lap to lie in a pool of golden sunlight.
Her athletic grace unmatched.
Her sense of poise never compromised.
Her balance an art form.

She licks her lips and luxuriates.
A lounging seductress.

-- Kevin M. Hibshman
(February Jellyfish Whispers)

Virgone

A kiss. Another.
A parting of cloth.
A parting of flesh.
Am I a Libra now?

-- H. Edgar Hix
(December Pyrokinection)

The Intelligent Design Café

you were probably wondering what happened
to life's first drafts, the rough sketches, paper models
and little cream cheese sculptures molded on the kitchen table
with a butter knife-you know, the ones with peppercorns for eyes.

you may have had a moment of sadness thinking
of the three-eyed people and the frogs with wheels for legs.
maybe you wondered about the squirrels with glass-clear skin
and rubber teeth and the whiskerless cats with radar.

well step right in you finished product you,
take a walk around the intelligent design cafe.
the place where the first drafts have a draft
and the dead ends sit chatting on their dead ends.

the Designer, it turns out, was a pretty decent guy
and he figured that if you worked for Him
you shouldn't get laid off. the distinction of extinction?
well, he'd leave that for the evo-devo darwinists.

and that is why this very day, in the intelligent design cafe
the influenza virus is bellied up to your cytoplasm with the virus that
only tells fart jokes and that all the people who believe
in the intelligent design cafe
can somehow breathe the same air as all the ones who don't.

-- *Lynn Hoffman*
(February The Mind[less] Muse)

Robin, beak full, streaks
across open sky; what radar
tracks which tree is home?

> -- *Sue Neufarth Howard*
> *(April High Coupe)*

Mamma walks the sky
at night sowing moonbeams...
seeds of poems.

-- Sue Neufarth Howard
(April High Coupe)

Wild, wet, naked joy;
oh to be five once again,
dancing in the rain

-- Sue Neufarth Howard
(August High Coupe)

Nigh Time

the clock in the piazza is fixed
at the same hour it was when
last I saw it
as I pulled away
from the train station
bound for Roma ...
almost one year ago

puzzled, I spend long moments
many - watching time,
waiting futilely for a change,
a sign
and in my mind I hear
a voice -
Ferlinghetti's insolent
chattering gets louder

his has been in the background
of all the voices for months
maybe longer
he orders up insurgency
without which he
warns, the end of things
is nigh -

he points to the clock
stopped long ago;
one more example
of certainty
in an uncertain world
you wanted to bear witness?
he is mocking me, I know...
bear this

-- S.E. Ingraham
(February Pyrokinection)

Big Toe

There were babies:
an armada of chocolate babies like the Luftwaffe
coming into view from the right side of the screen
in my head. The sky, the color of blood.
I could still feel the warm pulsing
where my left foot used to be.
I woke in sudden jolts
as if someone were shouting my name.
The room was blurry.
I tried to focus, tried to wiggle my big toe,
but the sky ran bloody again
and the babies were melting.

-- Jason Irwin
(February Pyrokinection)

Household

*Where can a blind man live
who is pursued by bees?*

   ~Neruda

Uncomfortable skin, incessant
itch to jump, to twitch, to hum

constant noise that gives him
hives–makes madness come

alive– a thousand wings fanning
figure eights until cells ignite

into fiery flight that burns
his eyes–tearless cries be-

come disguise, dodging
all that occupies his mind.

   -- M.J. Iuppa
   (July Napalm and Novocain)

Temptation in Standard Time

A fish hook moon skims
a dark city sky, promising
to return morning
without being caught

in a corridor between lives,
tempting those who love
the stolen split-second kiss
to linger in the doorway
that's damp with fallen leaves–
hard to forget, but
can't be remembered

Who were you, really?

And I, in spite of
purity, claimed your
unexpected embrace
long enough
to let it go

-- M.J. Iuppa
(July Napalm and Novocain)

Concurrence

Three days gone, the deer's
carcass disappears bit by bit–
its rib cage exposed in this

least-winter light– gleaming
within its chest like a stop-
watch, a sharp-shinned

hawk sits– unmoved by
the hum of traffic, looking
like radar, causing us

to slow down.

-- M.J. Iuppa
(April Jellyfish Whispers)

Moor

The autumn rains still lay across the moor, sheets of shining water under the moon. For days the sky had been clear and the nights cold, until the flood froze and the skating began.

Newcomers to the village strapped on skates, whirled and tumbled in laughing family parties. Excited children shrieked and mocked as their clumsy parents fell on the ice. There was no danger. There was no depth to this winter lake.

If anyone had been looking, they might have noticed that the old families, those whose grandfathers and great grandfathers for countless generations had worked these fields, skated in groups of men or women. Separate. There were no couples. And certainly no children.

Wordlessly they knelt beside the flood and tightened the thongs of their ancient bone skates. Only in a freezing year did they fetch these skates from their hidden place beside the chimney, rub them with a little goose fat, and carry them in silence to the icy moor.

If anyone had been looking, they might have noticed the figures cut in the ice by these skaters. Circles, arabesques, stars, triangles. The year the cobbler had tried to cut a pentangle in his scepticism, the ice cracked without warning. He fell through and broke his ankle. No one departed from the traditional figures again.

If anyone had been looking, they might have noticed the group of skating women fan out around a dejected young woman who stood in the centre of their circle. She had unlaced her skates and they lay like two beef ribs on the ice.

Round and round the women skated, faster and faster. The stars wheeled in their eyes and the cut ice swished under their feet.

With no signal, they stopped. It was time for the lifting.

The women moved as one towards the girl, who stood motionless, head bowed, waiting.

Strong hands seized her, and lifted her to the cold moon. Twice they raised her pliant body without effort, and spoke. *At Harvest.*

They lowered her gently to the ice. She strapped on her skates and rejoined the women in their silent circuit.

At Harvest, twins were born, and each child had a tiny sixth toe on the left foot. They didn't know why this should be.

It always happened with children born from the lifting.

-- Diane Jackman
(December Pound of Flash)

Frost

      onset of winter
I bent the back
 of an older man
to take a photo of

      a cobweb
wearing frost like
dangerous jewels
on   the path.

     but the light
was all   wrong
on   the forest floor
where beasts like this

blot out the sun.
and my knees
     indignant
at cold concrete

                 -- Miguel Jacq
                 (July Jellyfish Whispers)

Damnit, Roy

Would welding sparks hit the city
like tourists from the sun,
if not for Roy?

The city
a thought-pattern
of get-real blondes
dream drones
piss
in handbags
concealed
spin
abortions
balanced news
food carts
bike psychopaths
savvy suicides
radar glossy
Susan the weather girl:

Pole-dance tonight-
cloudy this morning.

Mammoth tusked Indians
quiet
as cigarette smoke
in dusty lobbies
playing backgammon
on a Turkish rug.

Lottery tickets
like cufflinks
on a stray dachshund
with 3 pieces
of photo ID.

Overpass noise
the thrill
rolling joints
on a diaper changing station
at your Mary's Dance & Dine
Broadway and Ankeny
girls girls girls
Visa Visa Visa
like soft wood rotating
on a lathe of Chuck Berry.

On the marquee:

A Pioneer of the Industry
We miss you Roy.

Yes, we miss you Roy
and no absolution
dispensed
by rainbows on skateboards
with fractured wrists
can replace you,
though the mayor is a Samurai
with bee stung lips.

                    -- Bill Jansen
                    (September The Mind[less] Muse)

McSea

that's the score on the tidal range
where water sizzles like chopped onions
where the sunset yawns like a pelican

where a boat slides on horizon grease
and I note the empty future of a crab
dragging away what drags it away

where rocks confident of their social reach
let mussels cling until they super size
and plastic toys burrow into hungry sand.

-- Bill Jansen
(March Pyrokinection)

Front Page

At the Bon Jour Cafe
a front page athlete
splashes into the *Oregonian*.

Plaster dust on my bagel
from a cupid shaped hole
in the ceiling.

The cafe is on 3rd Avenue.
A empty paper bag
floats across traffic like a single mom.

I ask the waitress for a new bagel.
Or a Lifeguard's whistle.

Then a bronze wet hand
rises out of page one
and steals the salt.

-- Bill Jansen
(December The Mind[less] Muse)

California Summer

Coastal warm breeze
off Santa Monica, California
the sun turns salt
shaker upside down
and it rains white smog, humid mist.
No thunder, no lightening,
nothing else to do
except sashay
forward into liquid
and swim
into eternal days
like this.

*-- Michael Lee Johnson
(October Jellyfish Whispers)*

I Am Looking for Something

I am looking for something
desperate within the shattering
of green glass, Coca Cola bottles made
entirely from grass, bark, corn husks.
Between rain, grey clouds, a spot of sunshine
cast on a shadow's fear
green grass sprouts, not grey bark
nor branches dead.
Truly, I am telling you,
I am looking for something
not the specking of rain
on my windshield,
nor the wipers that
habitually sling the drops
away, left, then right.
I am looking for something.
Exploring deist compared too theist
I was confused, an academic note
on the side plate of my day.
I believe in a God, but perhaps my God
is just an auto mechanic.
I think God is wrapped in a 4-leaf clover
sinless, searching Illinois farm lands for something.
Not in commercials, billboards, sales pitches, on the
highways, nor in text messages, double negatives hidden,
or the static of cell phone drama.
I find my Savior in the bluebird,
grasslands, scattered trees, slightly out of range.
Bring me a fluffed pillow, Wal-Mart special,
a dream of wine, vodka mixed orange
in a season lacking reason,
the bluebird flies.
Everything dreams and flashes away
I tell you something, I am looking

for something.
Savior bluebird.

-- Michael Lee Johnson
(December Jellyfish Whispers)

Empty Branch Trees

I am the purchaser of your life,
I walk in wild wind in late fall
dream sweet, dream often,
empty branch trees and leaves
look for you there.
But you are an isolationist,
baron, desolate, stark naked
tan buttocks touching shrine
on a half moon night.
You are worn like moth wings,
infected flannel with all ex-lovers
coming out of the covers and sheets
various men you have dated for over 30 years
men that now are a dash, some dead in time.
Sweet body builder,
alpha female your evaluation
of self-goes up, then down,
yoyo clumsy, temperature,
verbal disbursements
inconsistent with morning
sunrise and sets.
You orchestrate your life
tossing dice in dark
alleyways on south side
Chicago predawn streets.
Of the wings I displayed
for you, doves speaking
expressions in time for you,
wings beat in lost melodies
gone for all I account for,
nest to ruins, egg to shell,
the love once displayed for you
crow wings beat, blind my hindsight vision out.

Empty branches, memories gone,
highway emptied to hell.

*-- Michael Lee Johnson
(December Pyrokinection)*

Sunset in Morningview, KY

1.

Night
crawls - like
a toddler slowly scoots
toward curiosity - over the hills
that have become a shelter for the declining sun.

Light
fractures and
re-fractures into a million
shades of purple, pink, orange and red,
distorted by the wonderful atmospheric prism.

2.

Fires
burn hot in
the surrounding valleys,
sending the natural sap-tinted
smell of renewal floating through my nostrils.

Gardens,
newly plowed,
give off the scent of
fertile soil, as if the earth has
been ground down so finely that it too can fly.

3.

Chives,
fresh from the dirt,
taste like sweet onions,
causing my mouth to water and rejoice
in the bountiful flavors that nature has provided.

Tomatoes,
not yet ripened,
tease the taste-buds with
the promise of the juice induced
happiness that will come in just a few more days.

4.

Dew
falls like silent rain
over a bed of grass and
leaves that have parachuted from
the tip-tops of giant Oaks and ancient Sycamores.

Breezes,
gentle and comforting,
quietly gust and cause little
bumps on my arms and neck in delight
at the temporary relief from the valley's humidity.

5.

Coyotes'
harmonious howls
echo through the valley like
the violins reverberating in Beethoven's mind.
Crickets chime in with their chirps of up-tempo percussion.

Bluebirds,
and red ones alike,
tweet their evening song
as if wishing the world fruitful dreams and
giving a final melodic offering to the emerging full moon.

-- Ryan Kauffman
(September Jellyfish Whispers)

tequila sunrise
hangover at horizon
cherry, orange dawn

        -- Yasmin Khan
        (December High Coupe)

Found Poem: The Art [of the] Come-On: An Overheard Emoticon

student lounge. finals week.

her: i worked on the piece for 16 hours straight in an unventilated room. got high off my ass on turpentine.

him: you have a piece of glitter on your lips.

her: what are you doing this summer?

him: bookstore–d & d, coffee, comics–a dream job.

her: lucky. i'm saving for a new piercing.

him: i'll do your navel for 20 bucks.

-- Maureen Kingston
(March The Mind[less] Muse)

The Un-Found Poems

Duotrope's® 0.00% : zero calorie journals living on air : with no acceptances : do they really exist? : I mean : beyond the head of a status pin : beyond family and friends? : why of course they do : you say : but how can we know for sure? : the Pushcart® tells us so : (winners not nominees)

-- Maureen Kingston
(December The Mind[less] Muse)

***Sym-bi-otico:** A Notorious Liberal Bastion Prepares for the Fall Semester* (When God Closes a Door He Opens a Window)

beverage trucks back up to the student union
    (is it coke or pepsi school?)

bookstore clerks stockpile knapsacks
    (discover-visa-mastercard inserts inserted)

rope lines are staked for the frosh free phone pick-up
    (unlimited data mining access)

all-faculty memos flutter in mailboxes
    (re: the budget: no travel money this year
    unless you're attending a conference
    that teaches you how to raise money)

old signs are taken down / new ones put up
    (~~English Department~~ / ~~Humanities~~ /
    ~~Language Arts~~ / ~~Mass Communications~~ /
    Business School)

        -- Maureen Kingston
        (June The Mind[less] Muse)

Somewhere

Somewhere there are horses
loose in a canyon of clouds.

I listen for hoof beats wreathed
in silence, for whinnying cries

and the harmony of many colored
manes. I listen for the northward

flight of birds and all their rainbow
song. It's April and still snow

crowns every hill. Eagles fall
from the sky, feathery meteors

of hunger and lust. All over
America the auctioneers have

started the bidding for spring.
Money changes hands.

Somewhere there are waves
and dolphins leap through distant

surf. Somewhere whistles blow
and streams swell; tributaries flood

their banks. River towns hang
in the rising tides. Our bridges

are lost, they cannot hold; our canals
were never made to hinder the sea.

Waters thunder around our ears.
Somewhere a pebble rolls down a hill,

gathers dirt and rocks; whole mountains
shiver and skip and crumble into dust.

-- Steve Klepetar
(June Jellyfish Whispers)

My Forte

My forte has never been   chemistry
especially   in matters of the brain
this delicate science   eludes me
but give me a knife   and I'm a pro
a   butcher   in   a   cesspool   of
a   drowning   stagnant   me
where   the   water   under   my   bridge
does   *not*   flow   out
but backs up tighter than
               a meat packer's drain
overflowing with   bloody blobs of
broken   promises   and   good   intentions

                     -- John Kross
              (March The Mind[less]Muse)

(St) Ben(edict)

We have a cat named Ben who doesn't wear a collar
so he stays indoors.
I know a saint named Ben whose picture's on a medal
that I wear outdoors.

I wear it for the safety, a bigger one we hang above the door
for superstitious reasons like a black cat crossing our path
that isn't ours, Ben is ours but Ben is brown not black and
Ben won't wear a collar so he stays indoors.

> St Benedict of Nursia the patron saint of lots of things,
> of remedies for poisoning, of evil witchcraft, suffering,
> a patron saint of lots of things, of aggies, engineers,
> spelunkers and those with fever near the gates of death.

He is the patron saint of gall stones but not kidney stones
if so his medal would have saved me from significant pain,
but still I wear his medal when I go out to keep myself
protected from whatever it is he protects us against.

before he became a good luck charm, before he was a medal
he lived in a cave in Italy in the year 400 a.d. where for
three years the townsfolk brought him food to eat and finally
talked him into coming out. No, not that kind of coming out
he wasn't gay, he was a priestly hermit who was celibate.

They put him in charge of a monastery when no one else
wanted the job, but when he made the rules that still stick today
they didn't want to listen so they tried to poison him twice
both unsuccessful. This is where he gets the nod for sainthood.

Divine intervention saved the day, a raven stole the
poisoned bread and a spasm smashed the poisoned cup.
if they wanted him to go away they could have asked him
but I guess they needed a saint, someone to martyr, so
he went back to his cave and was promptly forgotten

until the Connecticut witch trials of 1647 when a captured witch confessed that her powers were contained by a conspicuous medal that she'd never seen before mounted over doorways, and she heard the whispers of the townsfolk say the medal was the medal of a saint they called St. Benedict.

I can personally attest that the medal is quite unique with Latin inscriptions on both the front and the back. On one side of the medal he stands and holds the holy rules, at his feet a raven and a broken cup. An inscription on the medal reads:

"May we at our death be fortified by his presence"

Flip it over and you'll see:

```
      C
    C S S
   N D S M D
    P M B
      L
```

"May the holy cross be my light"
 "Let not the dragon be my overlord"
  "This is the cross of Father Benedict"
   "yadda yadda yadda"

Along the outer edge it looks like this, strangely similar to a Ouija board.

```
           PAX
        B        V
       V          R
       I           S
       L          N
        Q        S
         M      V
```

PAX for *Peace*

The rest is this:
"Begone Satan yadda yadda yadda
 for evil is what you prefer yadda yadda
  so drink your own poison yadda"

350 some years since its inception and the medals popularity still flourishes. I reach down and finger the medal beneath my t-shirt and I realize what the strangeness feels like.

It feels like **witchcraft.**

I guess I'll wait and see if anything happens
before I pass judgment.

I hang it near our bed at night and while
we sleep

our brown cat Ben likes to bat it around.

-- John Kross
(May The Mind[less] Muse)

Wires Stripped Bare

Harder
Faster
Rougher
Thrusting ever-deeper into the mind
In the real world, I slowly fade
A tangible shadow of my digital self
Scare me
Hurt me
Push me past the brink
Her cries rain down in black and white
Fantasy is our new currency
Reality an unpalatable relic
Screams of zero and one
Tied and bound in binary
Submitting to illusion
The third dimension imposes fragile limits
Sensations no longer prized
A previously inescapable prison
Outside its walls the mind runs free
As the body goes limp and wanting
Scentless sex and senseless violence
Adrenaline rides raw on barebacked electrons
Until thoroughly spent and unfulfilled
A darker conquest calls

-- *Craig Kyzar*
(March Pyrokinection)

Corner of Abscess & Silk

                              (for Amy Huffman

slippage pour munitions wind

   -- the wound of demonstration –

glisten-gristle

grapple-grope

pustulance-shroud

                : bunch fibrillatives

                 fibrillatives bunching

bejeweling the lumber of still life

                          -- avalanche vortex

                          wind-catch

                          bristle-claw

clairvoyance shreds substance

cornering the altitudes of omnipresent delay

                  -- Heller Levinson
                  (January Pyrokinection)

Kazuya Yamamoto

I

Kazuya Yamamoto worked
at the sushi bar, cutting perfect
sashimi for the society elites
with their fat wallets and
ultra-gold credit cards.

They filed in and out, for 10 years
while he served them with a smile.

He seasoned perfect sticky-rice,
and trained others to roll it thrice
into little circles of perfect form
almost too pretty to eat.

II

Sally brought her little girl to
eat at the sushi bar. She taught her
to hold the chopsticks just so
and to spit in her napkin
when she didn't like
the edamame
and kanikama.

They came every Tuesday and
Thursday like clockwork toys,
the mother and the girl--smiling
with a barely recognizable konichiwa
before spitting out the nijimasu
in a neat paper napkin for two.

III

Kazuya saved the napkins,
in a leaking yellow ball
that sat quietly
on the window ledge.
He worked it with his hands
kneading it just so, before gently
slicing it into perfect circles,
and wrapping it tightly
in a nicely seasoned nori.

He served it with a smile,
saying konichiwa imi imishe kuso
and while bowing very low.

-- Glenn Lyvers
(November Pyrokinection)

How to Be Calm

If anyone asked, Ray would say, "The most important part of getaway driving is looking calm while waiting for them to come back. When they do return all crazed and hopped up, that's when you are your most calm. That's when you just go with it, whatever it is."

He remembered this as he waited down from the jewelry store. It was a big store. one of the biggest he'd seen. In his head, Ray began to list all the songs by the Rolling Stones that he could think of, which was his trick for looking relaxed and in his place.

The back door opened up and three people jumped in. They peeled off their masks and stored their guns and one of them barked, "Hit it."

Ray looked in the rear view window and then turned all the way around. "Wait a minute, who are you guys?"

There were three men, all who were strangers. The guy in the middle, with the long stringy hair, "Damn, we went into the wrong getaway car again." The other guys groaned.

Ray shouted, "What do you mean wrong getaway car? How many getaway cars do you think there are?"

The round guy on the left shrugged. 'I think there were three robberies going on when we came in. So maybe four getaway cars probably. It's a big store. It does a lot of volume."

The tall guy on the right looked behind him, "Can we get going already?"

"I'm not your getaway driver. Find yours, I'm waiting for my crew," Ray said.

The middle guy said, with a little panic in his voice, "I'm sure they'll be fine. There's always cars ready to book out of anywhere. Look around you, there's a ton of cars. So now you are in our crew. Let's go, you'll get your cut."

"But they are my bros, I've been with them for ever."

The tall guy said, 'Really your bros? They didn't look down on you? They didn't make fun of the guy with the car? They wouldn't leave you here?"

Ray turned back to the wheel and thought. His crew had three guys. Frank threw cigarettes in his direction. Jimmy called him an idiot grease monkey and Mike never even looked at him. His crew, looking for any convenient getaway car.

Ray popped the clutch and shot the car into traffic, going wherever you go when you need to flee.

-- David Mcpherson
(July Pound of Flash)

Chauvinist's Manifesto

There's a football field between us.
I'm in one of the end zones bellowing
and you're in the other one bawling,
the cliffs of your cheekbones
streaked with mascara.

Betty Friedan is screaming.
She says the problem is my fault.
Bella Abzug is cackling
that she agrees.
Gloria Steinem
is at the microphone,
ready to sentence me
to decades of marriage
with children by the score
though she didn't marry till 60.

These ladies must be right.
I'm just a man so I give up.
I accept all the blame.
Mountains have risen
in the middle of the field.
I can no longer see you.
And if I can't see you
there's no reason for us
to get together again.
I have to be able to see you.
It's always been your hind
and never your mind
that I favored.

We were having a wonderful time
and all of a sudden you got serious
like all the others.
They wanted to get married, too.
Listen up.

I'm going to announce
the best solution.
I want to be generous.
I hope you can hear me:
"You keep the ring.
I'll punt and go home."

-- Donal Mahoney
(March Napalm and Novocain)

Study in Fidelity

Breaking news:
Woman in a Cadillac
tries to run over
the husband
she claims is
a serial philanderer
and misses by inches.
She puts the car
in reverse
and roars over
another man
out for a walk
with his mistress.
The man dies
at the scene.
No word on whether
charges will be filed
or whether the widow
will testify on behalf
of the driver.
The women say
they're involved
in a long-term
relationship
both husbands
were aware of.
Details at ten.

-- Donal Mahoney
(November Napalm and Novocain)

Photograph, Age Eleven

In the photograph
the girl
wears a hard look
wound tight

standing by her bike
gripping the handlebars,
nearly eleven
about to peel her childhood off
like a wet bathing suit.

Her face says what she does not.

She is cautious
when the neighborhood boys call to her
to show her the fish they caught
in the lake. It circles and circles in the bucket.

When he places it on the board
and swings the hammer down
she jumps and learns how easy killing is.
The air is thick with chlorine and wet leaves
and she stares at the grass
stuck to his leg,
the hair on it turning dark, darker toward the thigh.
She tries not to look at the space between his legs.
It scares her as much as the now dead fish.

To think this creature just alive
now dead
forever
its mouth still open
almost calling to her.
Inside, her heart beats
she can feel it with every inch of her
but inside the fish, it is dreadfully still

and that difference is all she can think about
while she stands there, transfixed
doing nothing but trembling in her years.

> *-- Ally Malinenko*
> *(January Pyrokinection)*

The Car Accident, 1995

Yes, there was the scraping of metal
against asphalt
and the heavy low thunk of the Ford
lilting and tipping no longer bound to gravity
and then dropping with the combined weight
of all of our teenage futures.
But in stories I make it sound like it took so long

when in fact, it didn't.
The car was turned over in a fraction of a second,
sooner than any of us even had time to think about

and in reality I turned my head
to see my first love,
twisted and hanging,
limp against his seatbelt
his long hair over his face,

unmoving.

And I thought how young he looked.
How young we all are.
How young and bent and maybe dead.

Then I crawled on all fours out the busted window
like a sinner
away from the wreckage before anyone could speak.

-- Ally Malinenko
(October Pyrokinection)

Memory foam bed
Must have forgotten
I lost fourteen pounds

        -- Denny E. Marshall
        (June High Coupe)

Fifteen Word Title

Gordon has just arrived. He finds a wireless Internet connection and surfs the web. He finds a website that has open calls for submissions, for a drabble contest called "Why aliens do not exists". Gordon does not know what the term drabble means so he reads the guidelines. The guidelines say it is short story of exactly a hundred words. The title cannot be more then fifteen words. Hyphenated words count as one word. Gordon goes back to his spaceship and takes off. His thinking is, if they do not believe in me why bother writing a story for them.

-- Denny E. Marshall
(January Pound of Flash)

I Had a Dream and I was There

And every night she went to that sea and she saw herself

Free dancing foam
in my absent eyes of glass
Free evanescent skirt
in the white play of my wind

And every night she went to that sea and she saw herself

Life captured by the inebriation of freedom,
forever consecrated to the emotion of a Memory
Reflection of the last happiness hour,
born from the sea to flood my soul

And every night she went to that sea and she saw herself

White melancholy pleasure
through my rhythmic jumps downhill
Blue harmonic frenzy
through the depths of my moon halo

And every night she went to that sea
to drown into the timeless immensity
And she saw herself
inside the stable and fleeting totality

-- Alessandra Mascarin
(June Pyrokinection)

After History Ends

the survivors will gnaw bones and scratch in the dust
with sticks so meanings may live there tiny instants
like specks of seed in a forgotten sea

and night will dream its monochrome absolution
like an archaic priest who pretended
there was nothing with an essence

except one number; one, the number
of love and touching, the nothing
that comes

-- David McLean
(June Pyrokinection)

Virtual Love

A
long
slim
poem
full of hyperbole
& alliteration drifted
into the wrong e-mail box.

There she met an erudite
rich text format file.
They became attached.

Her fleeting metaphors
lifted his technical jargon.
They were a word couple
spinning through cyber space
giddy with inappropriate syllables.

-- Joan McNerney
(July Pyrokinection)

Shy autumnal bird
did you brush against the moon
to get that pale down?

-- Joan McNerney
(January High Coupe)

The Call

It's four a.m. and I'm in the office. Haven't been home for seventy two hours; big project at work. Need to call home. Oh, she knows I'm at work. It's just I haven't called in and have been here much longer than expected. Need to call home now.

Here's a phone. The buttons are small. I put in the numbers—damn, I screw it up—I put in the numbers again, and—damn, I screw it up again. This phone is just too small and hard to use. For some reason it won't let me use it. It doesn't want me to get through. My fingers turn all thumbs when I go to dial it. God damn it—I will find another phone.

Run downstairs and around the corner—go down the stairwell—there's an executive area there. It is 4 a.m. No one will be there. I go to the secretary's station—there's a phone—but it has no buttons! When I pick it up, a voice says Yes?

I need to call home—I need to call home now—

Please provide your passcode or the last four numbers of your social.

I blurt out the last four letters of my social—who the hell has a passcode—

Connecting, says the voice.

Silence.

Connecting? Connecting to what? I have not given my phone number. This is useless. I slam it down. I run through a long corridor to an area where there are many cardboard boxes stacked. There's a phone there—a dial phone—with a lock on it! There are many cubicles—many desks—many phones. I pick one up. There's a dial tone—and I try to type in my home number but I have the same problem I had with the first phone—I can't dial right—the keys are too tiny for my sausage like fingers. Time is passing—she's angry, I know she's angry.

Frustrated, tired of all this, I step into the living room.

She is going out the front door onto the porch naked, for all to see.

She is going to humiliate herself. I call out to her.

No—don't go out on the porch naked—

It's wrong to go out on the porch naked—

I will call—you will see!

You will see—

She goes out on the porch naked and bends over to fold some clothes she has laid out there. No! I cry—but she seems not to hear me. The sun beats down. I may as well not be there. I am not there, I tell myself—this is not happening—and at last my phone call goes through. I am leaning on a grey filing cabinet in a room teeming with people. I know she is on the phone but the din of the people makes it pointless. I yell I'll be home soon and she says something I can't make out—and I hang up, all impotent, turning a dark grey inside.

-- Jim Meirose
(January Pound of Flash)

Night is a Rarer Place

on Amazon rivers:
mirror of Mars,
of moon,
of the Milky Way.
Around a bend sleep
solitary three-toed sloths
in trees of dreams.
Mystery throbs in throats
of gladiator frogs,
Earth's primal drumbeats.
Keeping the ceaseless vigil of invisibility,
spectacled caimans watch
wide-eyed from deep time
in flooded forests.
The mind of darkness falls
prey to imagination.
Long-nosed bats begin to feed.

-- Karla Linn Merrifield
(April Pyrokinection)

Liver

The blood hole
in the white breast
is open to blue sky
& my brown eyes,
as the gull
of the gray back
& whiter breast
wields his yellow bill
to open another hole
in another murre,
another death for life.

-- Karla Linn Merrifield
(January Jellyfish Whispers)

Life in the Shell

Hungry Barn Owl chicks wait in the wings
of the shell of a theatre, never rebuilt
after a cluster of fire bombs played havoc
on the stage, the flames danced
through the stalls and balcony,
as the final curtain fell in the theatre
the biggest audience of its life
watched the act of mindless destruction.

Barn Owl parents in sophistic flight return
alula and legs extended, braking to land
under the roof that laughter tried to raise.
Prey hanging from curved beaks
ready to feed white heart-faced chicks
that look as ghostly as Hamlet's father
spotlighted by the rays from the moon.

-- Les Merton
(July Jellyfish Whispers)

End

We are right up against it
There is nothing we can do

War has been declared
The war to end all wars
is being over quoted
by the media and informed individuals

A conglomerate of planetary missiles
is set to be launched towards us
if the people of Earth
don't agree to evacuate
their beloved planet

Where can 7000,300000 people
of various nationalities, colours and races go

Yes a few - an elite few - will probably
be sent to various planetary outposts
some could even live on space stations

But, the majority
would have to stay put and just wait

There will be defences
The Powers That Be
have all missiles primed and ready

The end time
as been forecasted by many
over the centuries

Now it is a reality

Rather than wait for the destruction
The Powers That Be
have issued pills

the container they come in
is neatly labeled with the instruction
take three pills one of each colour
at hourly intervals
in the prescribed order

Take the Red Pill first
this ensures a feeling of well being

Next take the Blue Pill
it's sole purpose is to create a desire
for another pill

Which will be
the only pill left which is the Black Pill

It is very doubtful that before anyone takes the Black Pill
they will bother read the small print
which simply reads
END

-- Les Merton
(September The Mind[less] Muse)

In the Garden

        Eve reached
                beyond knowledge
                through icy leaves
                past imagination
                into shadow

her innocent hands
cupped succulent temptation

her body trembled
        she thought
        of Adam, of Adam, of Adam…

                -- Les Merton
                (October Pyrokinection)

Testicles, icicles
Everything hangs useless now
that it is winter!

> *-- John Miatech*
> *(March High Coupe)*

Zoom

Move cursor over nose, mole, waistline,
stray grey hair, camel toe
CLICK
Make bigger
until they become familiar allies
Soothing strands
to weave with
into collective patch
Fall in love with pixels
Magnification joins us
Bigger is OBVIOUSLY better
Pull back
into romantic distance
A medium shot
Feel the bonds loosen

Get closer again
Print out x-rays
Infrared exposes us in inky shadows
Husks filled with floating dinosaur DNA
A few have pristine diamonds inside

Only frame rare x-rays
Hang them in abode
Bravely heed them about once a year

-- James Mirarchi
(December The Mind[less] Muse)

Technicolor®

My clothes creak
Like the Tin Man's jaw.

Heels click on bricks
Washed yellow by the porchlight.

I think she's home, inside.
I brave the doorknob.

Yes, there she waits:
The great and powerful

-- Mark J. Mitchell
(February Pyrokinection)

Haiku After Santoka

full moon

an old man is peeing

on his own shadow

the destiny with no destination
the road is empty

frost on the ground
I cremate dead wood
in the cast iron stove

> *-- Suchoon Mo*
> *(January High Coupe)*

Sound and Sense

A distant horn honked,
defining the contours of
the outside city.

> -- *M.V. Montgomery*
> *(March High Coupe)*

Cold Hard Flash

the best western

    Two supernatural gunfighters face off in an Old Western town. Sundance is a vampire sheriff and Slim is a skeleton outlaw. *I want you out of town by sundown,* Sundance says. *I want you out of town by sunrise,* Slim says. *How about a drink before we get started?* asks Sundance. *No, no rotgut for me,* says Slim.

the bodyguards

    My bodyguards met your bodyguards and everyone got along fine. All the bodyguards wore their short-sleeve dress shirts with shoulder holsters and shiny wing-tipped shoes.

    Then my bodyguards and your bodyguards decided to play a game of softball. Afterwards, there was beer, music, and a barbeque. The bodyguards squinted at each other over their aviator sunglasses, teased each other, showed off their muscles, and bragged that their team was the strongest. A good time was had by all!

    Don't you think we should try to get our bodyguards together again soon?

the fake escape

    Two members of a Swedish gang kidnap a young unmarried couple. Grabbing their captives, they flee police by jumping from an impossibly high bridge onto a cargo ship.

    Later, the two criminals blend into the crowd in a foreign city, wearing yukatas, while the couple has escaped to the U.S. and is observed in a movie theatre, furtively embracing in the surreal glow from the screen. All appear to have found safe asylum.

Surprise ending, title: *They had all died in that initial plunge.* A shot of blanket-covered bodies on the deck of the slowly moving ship.

Well, I did say "impossibly high," didn't I?

fish story

At a fine restaurant, while seated out on the patio, I surprised my date by suddenly getting up and jumping into the goldfish pond. Then, since I was already soaking wet, I began splashing about and flapping my arms like fins.

Just stop it, she said. *Stop playing koi with me!*

just not done

I don't know about presumptuous, but it just seems downright unlucky to approach the captain of a cruise vessel and say, "Excuse me, sir, but what's your *cap size?*"

my relations with the cat woman

We had to be very careful, you see, because of my allergies. Difficult, very difficult. We had to kiss through tissue paper and avoid any direct contact with claws. I confess that I am a little squeamish in that way. And then I had to be careful not to say anything to send her spiraling into a hissy fit—yes, now, that's a pretty kitty.

right in front

I tossed and turned. I wasn't getting any younger, and when had been my last doctor's appointment? I did a skin check and was startled by a hard lump right in front of my face. But this turned out to be my nose.

spying on the neighbors

Over the years, I have been observing an elderly neighbor couple on the circle. Finally, I think my suspicions may be justified. The woman has been spreading out as she ages, her shape billowing like a melting candle's. The man looks like he is being sucked dry, his clothes hanging loose and his pants barely staying up.

Could it be—that she has been slowly feeding on him?!

wrong order

Trying out a new Mexican seafood restaurant. The host shows me to a table in a corner by the kitchen. A businessman sitting nearby greets me with a slight nod, then buries his face again in his *Journal*.

Imagine my alarm when two waiters suddenly burst out of the kitchen wheeling a large manatee on a gurney! They bump into the man's table, sloshing saltwater onto the fine linen tablecloth. Outraged, the businessman tells them, *I said, bring me a large MARTINI.*

-- *M.V. Montgomery*
(January Pound of Flash)

Dream Jobs

housebreaker

I was a housebreaker, but definitely in the wrong place at the wrong time, a neighborhood get-together. All the residents were paying visits to one another. It took me awhile to catch on to this and to realize that the sooner I left, the better. I escaped onto a back porch, trying hard to conceal a couple of small items I had stolen. I was greeted immediately by an elderly lady who said, *Oh, do you live here? I was just admiring your flowers.*

She painfully bent over to smell a rosebush near the porch, then asked me to show her around. So I started to take her into "my" home. From within came a friendly greeting: *Hello, who's there?*

He'll show you around, I said, and fled quickly.

beach clean-up

I am cleaning up a beach area, hosing off tables and umbrellas even though other workers stationed there do next to nothing. I am told by the manager, whom we all call "Mother," to find a rake, which I do. It isn't the best tool for the job because a fine mesh covers the sand. Only later, after scraping against the surface with the rake and accomplishing nothing, do I find another tool with plastic teeth like something used for cat litter. It pushes the sand back through the holes in the mesh. But then I press too hard and crack the handle. I am wearing sunglasses and a floppy hat: my late teen self. Next to the beach is a DJ stand where partiers wait impatiently for us to ready the area.

drifter

My partner and I were Depression-Era drifters traveling from town to town looking for any work we could find. We stopped at an open pit area, where our job was to get a box 1' by 6", fold it, label it with a number, then take it to the pit to fill with dirt.

Once filled, each box became a brick in a wall designed to keep unwanted immigrants out. We decided to quit once we discovered this wall: twelve feet high, three feet thick, decorated with a large skull.

angel in the house

Babysitting a young nephew. He was a toddler and acting up, apparently because he no longer fit well into his pants. So we went searching for another pair.

Then I was trying to finish reading some essays by Virginia Woolf and needed to find a quiet place. A crowd of people were hanging out in the kitchen. I took my book, spotted a bottle of gin, and thought I would sneak both back to my room. But en route, there were so many stray dishes and glasses lying around that I couldn't help becoming the Angel in the House and clearing them.

preacher

I am a black preacher-civil rights leader dressed in a dark coat and a wide-brimmed hat. Coming out of an assembly, I lose sight of my driver. So I begin to walk the few miles home.

It is a drizzly day, and I pause at a diner for shelter. There, I am accosted by a man wielding a knife who is on the verge of slashing me in the face. But the proprietress opens fire with a shotgun and the man's head explodes over my clothes.

not dressed

I arrive at my job as a factory janitor. The day shift still hasn't left; the place is full of workers in a festive mood, singing and playing guitar. In one area is a line of short Hispanic ladies being judged in a beauty contest. A gruff foreman approaches and warns me I am improperly dressed for my shift. I tell him I have a change in the duffel bag I carry and proceed to get ready. Then I am handed a pay envelope with little doughnut stickers glued onto it to reflect all the bonus hours I have worked. But I have never been paid, and most of the rings have fallen off.

poor prof

Only a poor professor, I found myself on the verge of being driven to prostitution to pay for an operation for a friend. When a student heard of this, he wrote me a check for $15,560 to cover all costs. In return, I took a vow of chastity and swore to become a monk. Twenty years later, I had many followers. Some even tried to buy me out of my vow!

-- M.V. Montgomery
(January Pound of Flash)

The Dilution of Memory

Embers fade,
disappearing into hushed night.

Petals wither,
falling on soft grass.

Words pale,
obscured by anguish within.

Faces blur,
dimmed by galloping years.

Kisses lose,
the urgency of bygone furnaces.

Feelings recede,
lying dormant in shielded vaults.

Love loses,
fatigued after numberless skirmishes.

Pain flees,
seeking new wounds to inflict.

Scars remain,
sentinels against,

the dilution of memory.

-- Afzal Moolla
(March Napalm and Novocain)

The Snake in the Pool

the little wriggler signaled with sun and water
distress and will to writhe
it acquiesced to my net
then examined the chlorine web on the grass with its tongue

it was a kind of snake I'd never seen
greenish with a big head

could be the sudden death of someone in a year

I released it because it was beautiful
because it wanted to live
because its ancestors slithered here long before the first houses
and I admired its ability to stay alive
among the fences, cats and pesticides

I would want a second chance
or even a third or fourth
if the world mistook me for poisonous
if I'd made some mistakes and trapped myself
in a pool of social and financial madness

                     -- *Bradley Morewood*
                     (February Jellyfish Whispers)

Mesoamerica

Playing parkour
with the souls in the street
the ghost of Musashi coasting
on an azure hydroplane-mirage

Sparse

Sunbathing sabertooths
hot bean paste cement
guacamole hair gel sorbet

My heart skips like stones
in a valley where bootleg orchards
bloom ransom notes
boast photosynthetic immunity

dry earth tangerine rust sponge
a sky whose black death
is renewed periwinkle

Chupacabras rest, serenading

Hotel Red Pepper is the only monastery for miles.

-- Erik Moshe
(May The Mind[less] Muse)

Summer Reflections

A particular boardwalk painted blue
challenges the sky for supremacy

afternoon suns heat the sands
and carry the sounds of children

splashing in the water
as small waves break

over a tan shore mottled
with bits of sea shells.

Time here hangs devoid
of impact or purpose

sunbathers are statues
in a gallery of sea life

there is no need to remember
and much desire to escape

the life that is marked by
mundane tasks and full necessities

the sun will keep all secrets
and only whisper to the stars

that nothing escapes the ordinary
orbits of space and time

not the heart, not the mind,
not even the sun, the sea, or the planets

held steady in the embrace of the universe
and the tempestuous calls of the infinite

-- Christina Murphy
(August The Mind[less] Muse)

Love Can Be

The last
   of the sun's light-
   gilding the lone bird's,
   flighty feathers.

Women
   whirling before-
   an inner eye, heads thrown,
   in an ancient movement.

Straggling
   across long-dead...
   faces, the mating dance,
   of African women

Like bees
   returning often-
   to their hives,
   our caves are still there.

And love
   can be a lonely-
   estate, of wounded seams,
   and tarnished dreams.

With messages
   Written on the

         -- Tendai R. Mwanaka
         (April Napalm and Novocain)

The Mighty Eagle

The American Motors Corporation (AMC) was bought out by Chrysler in 1987, but during the three decades of their existence, they gave us such wonders of the modern roadway as the squat yet spacious Pacer, the sporty AMX, and the off-roading Wagoneer. But no vehicle in their fleet commanded as much respect as the four wheel drive Eagle station wagon.

When my grandfather was looking for a way to spend his hard earned horse track winnings, he considered the obvious choices: Buicks, Oldsmobiles, even Cadillacs. But gramps was a man in the classical sense of the word, and he didn't have time for streamlined quality or aesthetic beauty. He wanted a machine that could burrow through the trenches of his trailer park when man-sized snow drifts would frighten lesser machines into dead batteries and frozen windshield wiper fluid.

The AMC Eagle wagon he purchased in 1985 had a tan, faux leather interior and a cream body complimented by coffee brown trim. It resembled a fossilized mushroom with an engine fused to the front of it, and after a few pumps of the gas pedal (but not too many, because the engine would flood) it would roar like a lion woken from a dream of drinking cocktails mixed with the organs of dead gazelles.

And upon my sixteenth birthday, the beast became my own. My grandfather had passed a couple years before, and the Eagle spent those lonely 24 months majestically rusting and dripping transmission fluid in our driveway. As I slid across the faux leather driver's seat, not as a child with a dream, but as a man with an ignition key, a bond was formed that would last through the remainder of my teen years.

The Eagle and I spent our mornings transporting friends to school, and afternoons waving to one another as I swung at softballs during gym class on the fields just beyond the parking lot. At night we would claim the streets, lawns, and medians as our own. From off road jaunts through the goal posts at my old elementary school, to dust storms created along the rubble of road construction projects.

Then one evening, the mighty Eagle would conquer yet another frontier.

We sat grumbling at a stoplight at the intersection of Golf and Barrington Road. The golden arches of a McDonalds added a yellow light to the orange glow of sulfur street lamps. My best friend sat by my side with two more friends sharing the back seat.

Then a Mustang pulled up beside us. It had the classic nineties shape, little more than a Taurus with sharper contours, but it purred with a souped up engine, or at least a souped up muffler.

I turned and made eye contact with the car's driver. A mocking smirk crept upon his lips. He seemed to find it amusing to be sharing the road with such an unorthodox creature as my Eagle. But I would have the last laugh.

I shifted my car into neutral and pressed the gas. Ancient elm trees knelt to the godlike rumble set forth by six cylinders of American made fury.

The Mustang howled in return, but the slightest trace of fear could be detected in its neigh.

The light turned green. I slammed the Eagle into drive, but pressed the gas slowly to keep her from stalling. We crept over the line with the grace of an ostrich, but the Mustang hesitated. Apparently, its jockey was inept at driving a stick shift. We roared across the intersection, leaving the whimpering nag in our wake, and clutching our fists in victory.

-- Adam Natali
(June Pound of Flash)

The Karl Rove of Checkers

My five year old grandson
is learning checkers
I try to slow him down
explain the strategy involved
Half way through the game
he reaches over and takes all his men
that I have captured
and puts them back on the board
"What's that?" I ask
"When a player wants to win,"
he says,
"and he has lost his men
he gets to put them back
on the board."
"O" I say,
"that's news to me.
I want to win too.
So I can put my men
back on the board?"

"No," he says,
"you don't get to."

-- Rees Nielsen
(February Pyrokinection)

wasps nests and prayer flags
a quiet co-existence
beneath the same roof

    -- ayaz daryl nielsen
    (December High Coupe)

Egret reflections
bounce on yellow ripples
between branches

-- Alex Nodopaka
(February High Coupe)

Seeking

In the ash-coloured dawn, I
have stared at the sequence of
petals, their ring.
To discover what will stand
erect as a tree trunk or lie flat
as the horizon.

The crimson-cheeked flower
possessed little knowledge of it.

I have gazed at the long road,
its endless hours rolled into
open-ended pouches.

A hope for something I
could hold up to the
light.

I have stood by the roadside,
no sparrows
twitter,
awaited the hatching of the blue-yellow-reddish
dusk.
Until my investigation
turned the gloved hand
inward. I dipped into me,

touched something equidistant
between the heart and the mind.
Something that could stand upright.
It was coloured

red by blood but absolutely
stainless. So, I knew I
could never find the shape of my tomorrow,

waiting by the roadside, gazine up at the
stars reading meaning into
floral patterns.

        -- Agholor Leonard Obiaderi
        (April Jellyfish Whispers)

Haunted

The flat still smelled of her
perfume. The coffee cup

held a red-crescent,
a lipstick memory of her
mouth

which formed a full moon
in happier times. Desire burned
the fiercest

when the moon acquired a
lover's round lips of ecstasy.
Mannerisms hovered in the air

like a cologne: the way
she threw her head back
to laugh at your scented jokes:

the way dimples formed moon
craters on her
cheeks: the method of

her smile that flashed silver
even in the sun's glare. But
most of all, the way she thrust

deeply into you
piercing, moaning then
leaving you marooned,

to stare at her dissolving
photograph.

-- Agholor Leonard Obiaderi
(March Napalm and Novocain)

Homeland

For you, my dear wise love,
for you I listen to Coltrane night and day,
adrift in improvised sound without words.
For your sake I walk on thistles and thorns,
broken bottles and mines.
For you I hold this distant fear that the earth will
erupt in fury releasing bones of friends and family,
sending me to hell before the bell tolls.
For you, my dear wise love,
for you I drink myself to sleep,
dreaming of your childlike folly:
the pranks you pull on fools, young and
old believers in your green and white promises
of plenty, of a blissful float above ground;
above lakes infested with worms.
For you, my dear sweet love,
for your sake my boom box overflows
with Fela's lament:
the saxophone cries foul,
the piano blames it on the drum,
it goes on and on and on and on
until I fall asleep,
until I am nowhere but in your cunning arms
ready to cuddle me,
to hustle me into oblivion,
to kiss me on one cheek and then drain
my dreams from the other ear.
For you, my dear homeland,
for your sake I bow before men and masks,
slip through cracks
and tether on the brink,
covering my face with the feathers you plucked
before I was weaned.

-- Timothy Ogene
(April Pyrokinection)

The Gift

I am trying to form a syllogism
but I can't turn the spigot on.

It begins with enormous loss
that crams you to the ground.

It takes months to dare to think
that loss is a kind of a gift.

But what is that gift exactly –
is it authority on the subject of pain?

What good is it to be an expert
on knowledge no one with ½ a brain would want?

What sort of gift is tears and who
would stand in line to taste them?

-- Turk Oiseau
(March Pyrokinection)

Cicada Shell *(a haiku string)*

She wants attention
just the same as the children.
Twining vines choke trees.

We have become one
of those couples without words.
Longing for mangoes.

Thirteen moons later
he leaves before I knew him.
No compass, no lamp.

-- Loretta Oleck
(May High Coupe)

in a few days
spring painted herself
ecstatic

        -- Mary Orovan
       (March High Coupe)

Lorca Deep Fries a Turkey

Whoever dreamed
peanut oil could change a life?
The first rule: never use
a frozen turkey.
Google it…a family moves
into the street in their stocking feet,
November rain like bullets, children
stricken, parents wide-eyed.
Through the dining room
window, as if orchestrated
by a surrealist, they watch
the table, crystal gleaming,
flatware polished, the antique tablecloth
catching fire at the corners.
The cook should have been reading
directions rather than Lorca.
He was back in Spain, fascinated
with flowers, challenging the heat,
his body a banquet
of fresh bread, mashed potatoes,
oyster dressing.

-- Al Ortolani
(May Pyrokinection)

Nineteen in '72

Sea-bright sand dune adorable midnight
ocean running mascara salting
my cellist fingers finding your note,
the small of your back l'Arc de Triomphe.

Do you remember that summer solstice
far far away from the madding crowded
envious bar in that Jersey joint,
freshman undertow tugging us down.

A name never asked, but what's in a name?
More, sweet girl, than ever imagined
joy, epiphany, wisdom igniting,
to be so young once more in your eyes.

Something unspoken, some thing not offered
but given, taken, not given, entwined
one kiss we surrendered shining immortals
these days, these winters, I cuddle your light.

-- Derek Osborne
(April The Mind[less] Muse)

Late in the Year

shelterless bird song
floats through rain,
darkens clouds

still, you can find me

the dandelions I dedicated to you
shine in wet grass

*

like young girls, one after another,
trembling --

each skittish tree
lights and rustles

under the sky's
reckless caress

*

still in the mind of the beloved
the leaf is trembling

green on the black branch
even after

this sky swallowed
the winter wind

-- James Owens
(January Jellyfish Whispers)

Air Passage

Like a ghost she speaks in a whisper
and her whispery breath flows
across my face like a desert wind, hot

whistling over carven stone and down
through narrow ravines
a whisper that makes my cheek itch

if you scratch it it'll only get worse
infected with some flesh-eating
virus and one word

that keeps repeating: *respiration . . .*
breathe in, breathe out
she murmurs blow out until your face

turns purple – when the spots in your
eyes begin to seem like old friends
you'll know you're almost there.

-- Jeffrey Park
(March Pyrokinection)

Animal Instincts

The cock crows at sunrise – a novel idea.
Here it comes, round and yellow
and warmth-giving like a brand new space heater,
oh boy, the excitement of it all!

Not like yesterday or the day before,
not like tomorrow or next Wednesday.
Ah, to share in his exuberance! In fact, I crowed
at daybreak twice last week myself,

just to give it a go. Didn't seem to work for me
though, like howling at the moon
or scuffing the smooth turf with my heels
or rolling over and over, just can't quite manage

to scratch that itch with compulsive
animal behaviors. Think I'll try
running circles around the porch light tonight.
See if maybe that does the trick.

-- Jeffrey Park
(January Jellyfish Whispers)

Bird Nests

Presents spring from tree roots
as gifts carved from stars.
Eyes are blind to baskets of bliss,

too clouded by the screen
of backstabbing and betrayal
to appreciate surprises built of brown.

Arms that support them never tire
or groan from winter's shake.
Wings of fire sculpt hearths,

insulating jewels of blood,
the new stars destined
to populate air's canvas.

They are intangible pillows
for hearts with dour prospects,
soiled gems for workhorses

during life's daily commute,
gracing them with reasons
to believe in hope and liberation.

-- *Lisa Pellegrini*
(March Jellyfish Whispers)

Revolution fails:
Men are pigs, and vice versa—
The poor remain poor.

> -- *Andrew Periale*
> *(January High Coupe)*

Our Collections

We started our collections with the
impasse and set our endowment in
sour satin. We mounted the byte chariot into
moonlight and let the dead worm fatten.

We praised the lump in the bend of the
neck and tied a corset round the coral
jury. We let the panorama fall strangely
silent and the square vent its fury.

When the syllable magnetized the encoded
caravan, not a gap refracted its darkening
value. But the pedestal equipped in taller
increments as all the panpipes went askew.

While the tropical family stood nonplussed in
rain, not a dining frog withdrew a quiet
slap. As the overflow and metric
garment dropped to a rambunctious lap.

-- Perry L. Powell
(August The Mind[less] Muse)

Mnemonic Peacock

Taller mown nebulae evoke strapped mothball stew, charging wounded martyrs with handheld rosin dumplings. Cowcatchers deplane at sunset, eyeing the romanced cloaking pigeon for signet hooves. Duchies imbue carnal divers with dolphin needs, elevating imperiled hooligans beyond Socratic wheelhouse blues. Clearance slicks balked satchels, creasing grim tirades, looped amid diurnal humpback engines. Hacked pudding empties dumplings of torn truculence, shifting mellow pheasants for sheaves of serried paltry nymphs, churning toucan peat. Glacial burgers seep melodic amethyst, clairvoyant in a worldly swordfish sort of swaggering gong. Pedestrian prints sleeve Studebakers in tunneled pterodactyl clues, prancing after midwife vows go unrequited. Daughters hover piously, cinching craven wolverines behind referral teething, granting eddies anoydyne deodorant news. Marking stallions plague astringent cardboard victors into licensed mirth, soiling egg tuners everywhere. Lonely muskets spin a vanquished caricature's snoozing periodontal fuse, crafting woolen giblets from slivers of impugned turbans. Browning features clash without dissolving antsy heels, pat down an execrable lupine fool, and ogle extravagant sundries, flipping barnyard anemones for choral fiefdoms sown to side yelps. Ivanhoe submerges for thievery's busty avuncular discharge, blubbering avowals to trained concocters of musical flares. Eyes hear rustling dish towels behind cold towers, keels untie angelic potions from strip mall fumes, and auxiliary coulisse mechanics fly sedan crops to destined missionary proving groins, clamping towel dregs to polar imposition. Dour forensic caregivers shock salacious lavatory salesmen, heaving gravy sires to face methodical heights of artsy capillary unguent's soothing pleat. Mateys swell to hefty slides of curried bleats, spooling sworn magistrates downtown. Wheel barrows erupt, spackling threaded placemats with skillets of familial pence, budging an oliphant in trafficked chrysanthemums. Healers perspire gear teeth, foaming groaty pores, sliming accordion tailings upon denial's clothed understudy. Betting on a rally, campers stomp as strangers munch in veering cherry walkways, giving hallmarks thermal tethers to verify crustacean samovars. Crunchy southern peacetime inches closer, tuning fanned dirigibles to sighs of loosely coiled summer, auctioned for anterior push-up housings. Callow ministers address egregious darkness, singing inner plugs of heirloom wharf reports, cresting in a moment's shuffle, penultimate and crowned with carousels of caramel and daisies. Seven hoed pairings devour arrhythmic yacht police, fending for disheveled unity, erring on the porcelain masthead's blotchy sawtooth weal. Herring induce lost flavors of ghastly delirium, flushing absent entrecotes in lamprey stakes of cooling plainclothes turbines. Christening a yak's boon with mashed attache kits, scraped stogies dribble salutary gnosis from shaven thirds of served dignitaries, dangling soiled actuaries in fallacious homestead ploys. An expectorant flies west for peacock backwash avoidance, sneezing cleverly, kissing mnemonic jerseys in sweatshop Pollyanna storms.

-- John Pursch
(March The Mind[less] Muse)

Aching Aloud

Heed the titrated otter's watery tribunal eyes before hive mentality erases the alligators from alluvial mentions of gumption and latitudinal anguish, pressed to varicose booties for playtime deities on nameless skeet coroner sheets of grassy carousels, driven to dribbling by hoarse beatitudes.

Splotches crocheted by gaudy iguanas in seething behest establish additional plumber humps from falling trouser commissary heaters, swearing haughty cisterns of huffy efflorescent teapot feet, scorching tabled integument with surreptitiously placated camshaft bricks, eating audibly.

Proxies intimidate cloaked events from aching aloud, shaving blurred cemeteries at drowning pole slides, kindling idiomatic synchrony for ossified seduction's glacine semester bonk.

Creaming stoned toenails with femoral lipstick gaggles, punchy slugs elaborate on dappled lancer steeplechase gloom, exposing polio olio in prawn retinue beach laments, soothing musty overboard tire irons before inducted tactile tallies can limp to brunch.

Moody blarings repeal salary haddock in pendant billows below orchestral gymnastic sleet, healing causal shamrocks on eiderdown elastic pleasure suits, munched and rosy.

-- *John Pursch*
(August The Mind[less] Muse)

The Magnificent Capacity of Two Fireflies

When stars flicker out, you want
to believe in reincarnation.

Maybe in another life, you'll be
a firefly, and I'll be a moth

following, drawn ceaselessly
into your light. Or perhaps

I will chase you like daylight,
follow from the in-between.

Or I'll become a firefly with you
so in untainted darkness, you'll find me

still believing the wisdom
of white flames and gas.

-- Jenny Qi
(December Jellyfish Whispers)

Beggar

When I listen to him, all things are possible. His voice, so throaty-rich, so pure. I think of Jesus on the cross. Life becomes smeared light, death a dark-blink interlude. *Dear God*, I think. *Dear, sweet God, make us better, make us free of the blame that holds us back, take from us the violence that squeezed us from the womb. Dear God,* I think, *dear sweet God.*

A final strum on the battered guitar, and his song is finished. I reach out. Notes tremble on the breeze. I want to hold them to my face. I want to make them real. Dust falls from my fingers into the slanted light.

He picks up a beret holding a few dollars and coins. His skin is dusky. "You like?" he says. He jingles the hat. His fingers are callused, half-moon fingernails stained.

I turn my pockets out. Coins spill onto pavement, a key ring, a pack of gum. Quarters bounce and roll through tight spirals.

His expression does not change. I take my wallet out, and dump it too. Bills flutter down, credit cards and business cards. The sidewalk litters with my life.

Still, his face remains impassive.

Tears come into my eyes. "Is that not enough?"

He watches.

"It's all I have," I plead, "all that I have with me. Please, tell me it's enough."

He pulls a cigarette from his shirt pocket, and presses it to his mouth. "Do you have a match?"

I pat my shirt, squeeze the cloth ballooning from my pockets. "No, no I don't."

He leans the guitar against the building. "Come back when you do, okay? I play again."

"Yeah," I say. "Sure." It's never enough. I never have what I need. I start walking. A breeze pushes from the north. I shiver. I look back.

A crowd has gathered around him. They jostle for position. I want to understand that they're after the money, but in my heart I know it's more than that. They're cleaning the ground of my residue, preparing for someone more worthy.

-- Stephen V. Ramey
(August Pound of Flash)

Sometimes

today
in the mucky midst
of your delicious deceit
your coy dog smile
was like sack full of dead kittens
on a wood and feather altar
to the Lord of Futile Fuckery
who was worshiped
circa bone nose rings
by ancient hunchback assholes
who ball-busted their spouses
to make it rain.

and they really needed rain.

an you really slit me open
sometimes.

(my affection is bleeding out
like a bruised sunset)

-- Niall Rasputin
(February Napalm and Novocain)

Mourning Walk

I bare-pad down
the zig-zag path
of broken laughter
and glowing-hot screams

breathe razorblades
cry buckshot
piss magma

stop by your plaintive grave
to remember why
and where I'm walking

this rancid world
without you
is not fit for maggot
nor man

just keep moving
toward the bastard sun
until he gets spooked
and swallows
me whole

then, we'll dance victory
in that voluptuous molten belly
like ghost-dog gypsies
and start our dream
over again

love and meanness
are fireproof

                     -- Niall Rasputin
                     (February Napalm and Novocain)

Snipers in the Sun

Wiping the sweat from my brow, I crouch lower behind the small, upturned car. My enemy's out there somewhere, but where? Slowly, very slowly, I edge forward to have a peak around the side of the car when... WHAP! My back arches at the cold, shock of impact. I've been hit! I've been hit! But how? How did he get behind me? Falling to my knees, I desperately try to return fire. But nothing happens. It won't shoot. I'm empty.

'You win that one' I shout with a grin before running to the tap for another refill.

-- *Chris Redfern*
(November Pound of Flash)

When You Cross the Street Like a Sailor Breathing Underwater

there's something about
the
cold
and the
sadness of winter
that makes
a cat curl up
and
makes my hands
curl up
and makes everyone in the world
long
for someone else in the world and
yearn
for something else in the world
    something more in the world
so I listen to your voice
until I fall asleep
and it's spring

-- Laura ARojas
(August Pyrokinection)

A Geisha Reminisces Over an Illicit Love Affair

On leap years,
we used to romp through oriental gardens.
Such slipshod footing, lovers tumble headfirst
from airy gables.

We were blind,
our eyes congealing from the star-smeared visor
that once held a promise for the future, one
of tortured romance.

But instead,
our passion soon deteriorated—
An ancient scroll with burnt tea stains, frayed tassels
eaten by silk moths.

Only now,
do shadows weave between the green bamboo thicket,
where hibiscus flowers loll their citrine studded tongues
like a yawning corpse.

Drowsy gnats.
Shapeless mantles of light suffuse a pond's dark edge.
Puffs of white mist float like Chinese lanterns,
a moonlit paper nest

for swallows.
Mirror-scaled koi flick their whiskers at the sky
as water sloshes over a lipped-rim bowl of clay,
nourishing silt.

Red crowned cranes
stalk the muddy banks in search of a lost mate.
Long necks stretch, trill cries erupt into the night
unanswered.

Wind-cradled
cherry blossoms litter the small pagoda
where our hearts bled into rose tinted vials.
Mingling souls

but keeping bodies apart.

-- John Roth
(September Jellyfish Whispers)

Dehydration

It starts with a dry spell,
a nagging cough,
and soon becomes
a burning hole
in one's throat.
The desert gargles
sand in its mouth,
picks the blisters off
its scorch-split tongue.
If only it had tears
to spare, some hidden
reserve of water kept
deep within itself.
Some way to taste
of its own sorrow.

-- John Roth
(September Jellyfish Whispers)

Quench

The sun hangs low
like a gold medallion
looped through a blue
prize ribbon.

There is nothing
to be won but red dust
and desert flies, rubbing
their greedy legs together
like dull violin strings.

A stone-painted lizard
sleeps flat on a pillowed
rock bed that's been drunk
bone-dry by mouthfuls
of burning sand.

The land cries out,
then comes
a noiseless surge
of black-bottle storm-clouds,
descending from the splintered
planks of sky like anchors flung
overboard.

Then comes
white lightning, shackled
to earth's hot ground plate.

Then comes
the calming hush of rain.

-- John Roth
(September Jellyfish Whispers)

Hirsute Fantasy

Hair sloughs like snake skins
In piles on the pillow, fashion
Auburn berms where dreams hide
In petite oases of the mind.

In morning, the gatherers
Count them like sheep
Baaing relentlessly at the loss.
Shimmering tracks of emptiness

Lay there in Saharan deserts.
Hairy sentries left behind, nomads,
Find a final resting place
Wadded in toilet tissue.

Comb overs hide the wadis
Visible when the sun shoots
Rays through them.
From behind mirrors capture them

Brown dot sun-mound, a camel, rests
In that desert waiting
For the others to jump ship
Before hair spray attempts to holds them hostage.

-- Sy Roth
(February The Mind[less] Muse)

A Bifurcated Road

Indifference nestles between the sheets.
The two poles roll over
and mumble hasty *goodnights* sometimes,
passion a long-forgotten puppy-dog romp.
Sensuality replaced by time,
waxy faces and bloated bellies.

They are reality stars
without substance and they fill empty spaces.
Desire, along with the dust bunnies,
swept under the bed,
replaced by C-Pap-induced memories,
an etude of Siren-slurping susurrations,
nightly hissed asps in the darkness.

They dress in their closets.
Bed partners who reside indifferently
offer comforts in dram-sized measuring spoons
papered over by blank, colorless dreams.

-- Sy Roth
(January Napalm and Novocain)

Avatars Dissolve on the Wind

mountains of them,
breathless idolaters
linked under an umbrella-blue-sky,
hundreds like underwear crammed in a suitcase
helter skelter compost piles of them,
caterwaul encouragement,
medal bearers lavish them with gold,
      silver-capers drape them,
            spring's leaden warm air lulls them.

festivities buried beneath
an ear-splitting smog
breath whisked away in a screaming chariot
calm adrift on a madding sea,
reduced to pulpy street dross,
limbs afloat in a wind of howls
cordite-choking cloud
a shroud.
vermilion walk of fame stars mark their being.

avatars dissolve on a wind of desiccated truths
under the blue umbrella
before piles of limbs
and streets to be washed
dressed in a soft-down of teddy bears.

                -- Sy Roth
              (June Pyrokinection)

Three Times Thirteen – Black Balloon, The Kills

Quarter pounders,
a full plate of coleslaw, soda
chips, crisps, chocolate coated biscuits,
snickers, Mars bars, sauces, saucers of gluttony.
The food you eat is not the one that will sustain the corpse you bear.

The grey veil covering the sky is your worst enemies in the mourning.
He was a chef, an artist, gardener, she wrote it.
Did he believe in God more than he
ever believed in you? You
will never know it.

-- *Walter Ruhlmann*
(August Pyrokinection)

1515 13th Street

When my father died
We moved to the Hill Country.
And when my aunt died
We moved to Lubbock.
Blue Northern from the Panhandle
Blinding dust storms out of the West.
My mother's other sister
Was our keeper and provider and we
Were not unlike prisoners.
Me in high school.
My mother sick in bed.
The house was a two-story red brick
Rooming house with a Church of Christ
Behind and a funeral home cater-corner.
My aunt kept her deceased husband's
Bible in a closet that like a refrigerator
Gave me a place to go
And look as though
There'd be something to see
Or someone I could maybe talk to.

-- Weldon Sandusky
(December Pyrokinection)

The Point of Picking Berries

All for a handful of berries the walk
sidles up the mountain top on paths
beaten by boots and occasional trucks.

Hikers and cops, bicyclists and hippies,
whole families from the cities now astray
playing One Of These Things Doesn't Belong Here.

Nothing belongs here but the berry clone –
a single shrub that seems to be thousands,
and covers acres, and which draws us in

where anything hungry could watch for us,
including this plant whose fruits seem to lead
ever farther from the trail and the homes

from which we often drive to shop for berries,
never fearing the bait or the hunger
we feed because it seems to be our own.

-- M.A. Schaffner
(April Jellyfish Whispers)

It All Comes Down to Investment Strategy

A little putty, a little paint, and life
just doesn't get any better, though death
is just as feared. What's more, the more you have
the more you burn on sleepless nights tossing

thoughts like flaming candy, weighing prices,
penalties, and cures. One never gets too old
to never want to give up anything:
dreams of houses with undiscovered rooms,

waking up thirty years younger and just
as wise or rich or not, though it's OK.
Even the pope's shoes seem simply tawdry,
even the pyramids a waste of time.

-- M.A. Schaffner
(May Pyrokinection)

lonely ocean wave
long travel completed
in a sandpipers retreat

> *-- Carl Scharwath*
> *(February High Coupe)*

Memory Pillow

"Sleep well?" she asked.

"Yes, but strange dreams," I said.

"How'd you like the memory pillow?" she asked.

"What? What's that?" I said.

"It conforms to your head and neck," she said. "It's my daughter's. I took it off her bed."

"Has she been to Tzfat?"

"Yes, it's one of her favorite places. Have you been?"

"No, but I remember it now."

-- Ken Seide
(May Pound of Flash)

It Was There

10/27/05 Three Days after Hurricane Wilma's Strike: Remembering Her Power

It was there by the burnt light, by the gaping wound in my mind that I saw inside my body, curled like a fetus with my eyes open in fear.

It was there by that hole in my soul that I saw my white bones carried away far into the sky, and my heart up on a fallen tree with tears of sap in my open veins.

It was there by the silence of my bleeding eyes that I saw the land carried away like a broken toy, and me as a little boy drowned in my cry.

It was there by my dry mouth that I saw the birds fly deep into my chest, carrying me out of myself into the wind, howling in the white of its pain, drowning into the black of its eye, falsely so calm.

It was there where all that was left was the flickering light of my soul, soul made out of stars and of clouds, and the incessant void.

It was there that I cried with no eyes, that I spoke with a severed tongue held in my bleeding palms, and I shattered in owe as the pressure declined and drew out my lungs.

-- *Dr. Ehud Sela*
(May Pyrokinection)

The Absence of Silence

Today the cuckoo will stutter and hover uncertainly
as it sings the joyous tidings of the new dawn.
The tribal women will hurry past the closed gates, heads bent,
for his quiet smile won't greet their mischievous mango-stained laughter.
The baby next door will gurgle expectantly for Nana,
as she stares out of the window, only to subside into a woeful quiet
that requires all the comforting powers of her mother.
The squirrel won't come out of its nook, only stare,
with dim, beady eyes at the once well-fed street dogs, wandering aimlessly.
The passersby will hesitate as they cross his gate,
their mouths opening in greeting. Then they will briskly walk away.
He has gone now. He has finally left the sun-baked red soil well-trodden by his feet.
This fall, you won't see him fragile and bent,
slowly picking the strewn leaves of gracious old Dorothy,
only slightly younger than him.
We knew him not, whence he came from, his age.
He was as timeless as the rippling brook flowing from weathered rocks,
greeting generations of passersby with a gentle morning nod.
We knew his presence, we knew the soft silence
that greeted us as we passed his gate, his cheerful eyes making us feel secure
No more…

The village is silent and ill at ease with itself. The silence is tense and heavy.
And the young white-clad woman tries to push away the violent stillness
Attacking her as she softly covers her father's withered face.

-- Adreyo Sen
(April Jellyfish Whispers)

Village by the Sea

The discordant symphony of water and pebbles
ushers faint whiffs of the Raat Ki Rani.
A distant rumble rolls through the tense skies
as a white streak passes across the velvet blackness,
only to vanish in silence.
The sea roars back, stormy waves surging forth,
its enraged froth fast drying on the parched white sands.
A dull yellow blur grows larger along the mountainside,
revealing the centuries-old path of lovers.
Her ebony hair and clothes plastered to her skin, a girl calls out,
to the scattered white specks, her eyes smiling.
They come together in a final sonata of cowbells.
In the scattered mud houses, the black-red stoves
burn steadily to prepare the night's meal.
The cicadas pick up their personal quarrel,
stilling the night with their evil shrillness.
And as the last glowing embers of a long day slowly fade out,
The far away city's giant causeway of ebony-stained yellow lights
Is reduced to empty darkness.

-- Adreyo Sen
(April Jellyfish Whispers)

Hands

the fool on the hill, has taken up residence in my head.
& then on the couch, smoking my lungs blacker each
drab day. my fool eats whatever is thrown close enough
but the best cuts of meat are thoughts & hands. the same
fool who, with best intentions, led me to bickering
relationships with women, drudging days of bank
work, microwave nachos & regular day long *arrested
development* marathons, which made me question life.

that fool takes my hand, searching through stacks of un—
educated this & that. & is always sure to keep me
comfortably uninspired & like wrists hog-tied to a couch.
it's only when i drive, alone from the bank, my head
becomes clear, & music cha-chings from ear to ear, as if
my black jeeps cab creates some kind of homebase.
inevitably the needle scratches the record & my fool

comes to mind. driving thirty-five down twenty-third
takes the piss out of me, i pass homeless like they were
starbucks. the music now sounds dull & the thoughts
stop. only thing coming to mind whether or not to take
mom up on the offer & call doc for free anti-depressants.

that & the bums. i bet they got some fools too. click—
clacking fool's voices in the ears of every busted home—
less on street corners, highway exits & barhall parking lots,
who i refuse to pay out for fear a buck less brings me a
step closer to them. these hands, when i drive alone, ache
to collect my thoughts, yet at the end of everyday are

stuffed sweating through the denim of my pockets, or
demolished between my ass & a couch cushion, while i
stare up at the ceiling fan on hi, like a fool, focusing on
each blade, tryin' to figure what i should already know.
barhalls & banks have little to do with hands. cigarettes &
couches have little to do with hands. knowing this

all thats left to do is flip the fuckin' fan the finger
& get on with my day.

>*-- H. Alexander Shafer*
>*(April Pyrokinection)*

In the Absence of

My sisters invaded the bathroom
        with a video camera
        while I was pooping
        They weren't recording
        Now I always lock the doors

I'm never sure what side to stand on
        in sandwich shops

I didn't hold her hand as we walked

        In school
        we always
        talk-piss
        Yesterday
        I wasn't
        ready
        & neither
        was he
        so we held
        our cocks
        with occasional beeps
        from the automatic flush

        This is how I feel about saying
        Dad

        -- Matthew Sharos
        (May The Mind[less] Muse)

Hawk, Poised

World-viewed incandescence; sun under his wings with last quick volley, slipping through a hole in the sky, lilting the soon-gray aura without a sound, an evening hawk appears above us. From Yesterday he comes, from Far Mountains only Time lets go of. Under wings steady as scissors a thermal gathers, not sure the joy is ours, or his. It flings him a David-stone, racing the Time-catch at heart, at our throats. There is so much light falling down from him, from wing capture, we feel prostrate. To look in his eye

would bring back volcano, fire in the sky, a view of the Earth Earth has not seen yet. In apt darkness chasing him, in the mountains where gorge, lake and river give up daylight with deep regret, his shadow hangs itself forever, the evening hawk sliding mute as a mountain climber at his work, leaving in our path the next hiker's quick silence, stunned breath, the look upward on a frozen eye and a drifting wing caught forever only by light

-- *Tom Sheehan*
(April Jellyfish Whispers)

Of Trumpet

☩1☩

spoken glass this dancing
angled area
broken
                        gregarious
aspects   wholeness now more whole
dedicated showering shine
scraped but bountiful
beautiful language of shards
detecting multiple

insinuation

calibrating balanced sighted versions of
fractioned momentum of sight

                -- Felino A. Soriano
                (May Pyrokinection)

Delineated Angles This Odonate

swelled the swollen ring

       halo ontology
       flame in the blued momentum
       figurative, pre-, though slim halls are
walking into widening varied interest
                                the
blur resembles foreign syllables
in the hover of waiting for
language to conceal uncontrollable
virtues

                -- Felino A. Soriano
                (July Jellyfish Whispers)

On (a) Reacting to Her

—*for my daughter*

I met you amid a photograph's earlier presentation profile

contouring into explanation of your face's familiarity

       the hybrid of grays engaged hanker to
view prophecy of the finished becoming (ulterior)

       perhaps the oval frame of the months' teaching (waiting)s

would interact with the artistic dimension of language's valued
personal excitation…

       -- Felino A. Soriano
       (September Pyrokinection)

She Wore a Marigold in Her Hair

She wore a marigold in her hair
-the country bumpkin amongst flowers
its artless, summery grin
trying to add a sparkle
to her fickle pansy smiles.

Once she'd worn orchids
braided in those silken depths
in exotic swirls of perfumed poetry,
when herself a lyrical sigh gazing at life
with wide almond-eyed naiveté.

She is a fistful of words
that she sings in fractured lines,
her croon a stilted echo of the obsolete
its fragments glued by self-concocted phrases~
just to hear vestigial vocal cords
croak out strings of hollowed syllables.

Her existence bracketed between
grocery lists and petty dinner table woes,
whistled urgency of cooked meals
the only noise bursting into her daydreams,
she whispers comforting words
to herself just to fill the emptiness
that yawns betwixt
clothesline trysts in the sunshine
and sleepy lullabies crooned
to the howling crib at midnight,
while her fragile sleep is
oft lulled by snored indifference.

Love is like wallpaper
carefully chosen and then just existing~
a dried rose once treasured
within sepia pages of mottled reverie.

It is revived at times in echoed smiles
or a softly whispered peck on eroded cheeks-
a firefly kissing fate-lines on palm
before twilight loses
its transient grasp on acrylics
and night intervenes...

-- Dr. Smita Sriwastav
(December Pyrokinection)

She Murmured Her Angst to the Silence

Sorrow: found herself
a fistful of metaphors in ~ tempest smudged skies,
a deer in deserts chasing mirages,
a bruise staining an ache,
colors erased by twilight's washcloth,
rain-withered rosebuds,
a festering cry of barren womb,
vacant eyes of orphaned innocence,
autumnal penury of deciduas,
tarnished December sunshine.

Sorrow: is the season
~ a lingering shadow; a fragile sigh
between russet autumn
and laughter of a summer cascade.
The murmur of a dream losing itself
in concentric ambiguities
of onion-skin slumber.
Sorrow: a whisper between
flimsy winter mists, its
gloomy syllables voiced by snowflakes,
falls in commissure between night and dawn
when even stars have dozed off
and the moon is fading away.

Sorrow : the grit left after joy slips away;
the sigh gasped when helium balloon
of transient bliss escapes~
a floating bubble bursting into soapy sprinkles—
just another face
of emptiness, loneliness, longing…

-- Dr. Smita Sriwastav
(December Pyrokinection)

Harlequin Whispers of Night Sky

moonlight is
a soothing, serene drizzle;
starlight sparkle of
sepulchered memories,
constellations crotchet
a refulgent veil.

stars wink
ancient anecdotes in
ambiguous stardust scribbles
within blackberry silence.

psychedelic sighs
echo in abeyant moments,
as photon whispers
knock on indifferent eardrums~
too entranced by moon's serenades
to interpret them.

-- Dr. Smita Sriwastavl
(December Jellyfish Whispers)

Father May I

come inside he said
rubbing his beard
with his third right knuckle
let's make confession

He ushered me in.
He sat me down.

he glided in one door
I fell through another
we separated
by sliding the screen.

He slid it back open.
He reached for my hand.

his tongue fondled his palm
his palm pressed into his cassock
I saw it
and gagged

He wiped my spit.
It became his own.

                     -- *Melissa Steinle*
                     (February Pyrokinection)

Landmass

There is a lone stack
standing out at sea, a sad
promontory that's jutting
beyond the riptides. I often
watch it and wonder why
there's only one, because,
surely if it was formed by erosion
there'd be more along the coast
This is a desolate beach to walk along
and when I go there by myself, I try to
imagine that under the surface of the water
the cliff and the stack are touching, holding
onto one another through the swells, and
though the peaks and troughs will do their
damage, what is under the surface will
never be erased, and never be separated

-- Leilanie Stewart
(December Jellyfish Whispers)

Snowball Effect

I'd like to introduce you to
Miss Lauren Tide
She came all the way
From Greenland
And is planning to stay
for a while,
an epoch perhaps.

She'll be bringing along with her
Miss Tundra, Miss Glacier
and Mister Permafrost

She was forced to emigrate
from her home, up North,
by convection currents-
hot air brought on by CO_2

She'll cool the seas before her,
Push the Gulf Stream further south

It's a waiting game now
for the snowball to come
She'll wipe out the arrogance
of humankind, with one swipe
from her terminal moraine

-- Leilanie Stewart
(December Jellyfish Whispers)

Twenty Questions

"I can't get it. I give up!"

Andy stared at his wife. "After nineteen questions?"

"It's impossible with you."

"What's that supposed to mean?"

Shirley smirked. "You should know."

"Huh? How is 'belly button fluff' any harder than 'naked mole rat'?"

"See? It's always a war with you – I'll never win. You think of the most obscure topic."

"You could've played along – for just one more question!"

"Played along? Forget nineteen questions; this was nineteen years – of hell!"

Shirley got up. Nineteen years. After nineteen years of marriage, a nineteen year old wisp of a girl had got between them. He didn't know she knew. He liked to play games. He wouldn't win this game. She wouldn't let him.

Nineteen questions. Nineteen years of hell. A nineteen year old girl. Nineteen steps to the door.

"It was only one more question," Andy yelled.

Only one more step. Shirley walked out the door. She shut it hard behind her.

-- Leilanie Stewart
(May Pound of Flash)

One Hundredth Meridian

Where the West begins:
mountain slope frontier
where the tall grasses end,
the first rise of red maples
after the treeless death plains
they walked through for
months losing cows and
children, the old and weak

and inland there is no beginning
or end
there is only light, dust and red
rock in endless mazes
invisible rivers below,
wooden fences wavering
into a heat-warped distance
the center of the West
doesn't know its boundaries--

cold deep waters
    warm shallow seas
        the small creeks draining
        the bluffs eastward.

Where the West ends:
at the ocean's lip scattered
with driftwood, sheer cliffs
brooks alkaline from the redwoods'
roots hiding under sword ferns
and alders in the dim mists,
sea stacks and natural bridges
elephant seals sleeping
in a bright sun, dried kelp
before a deep canyon in the bay,
harbors facing only toward sunset

the sand reflecting a setting moon
leading off the edge of the earth.

-- Emily Strauss
(May Jellyfish Whispers)

The Wind Hits

The wind hits in tight fists
like a boxer, circling, quiet
then suddenly striking from
the north, now the east

it fools me when I set a cup
down, unfold a chair
it doesn't like cups—
that's in the bush—

or chairs— that's knocked
flat, or dish towels drying
or wash basins— the soapy
water flies into my lap.

If I were more patient
I could out-wit the wind
dodge its icy punches
eat warm food, watch

the full moon rise over
the dark desert. Instead
I retreat, let the gusts bow
my tent like an accordion

a cold bellows, not for fire
but a sub-zero night.
I wear four layers to sleep
and hope for daylight.

-- Emily Strauss
(May Jellyfish Whispers)

Promise of an Eagle, to a Friend

for Rita Hartje

— *Sin & Confession*

You've asked me to speak of eagles.
Of diurnal flight over moonlit valleys.
I was to offer you the brazen talon
of its faith, hope, and love. As a song.

But I lied when I said I could spring
this bird from my heart willingly.
I betrayed myself into thinking
I was the keeper of its valor. I am not.

In truth, it flies through me but doesn't see me.
A ghost of old tears reflects from its eyes.
And though my soul is wretched and my ego has lied,
I long for your unconditional love. In dreams…

So many nights I've fallen asleep in your heart!
Awoken in the world your words have built.
I can't kiss your angelic face, but I hear its soft music.
It sings that our distance is illusion. It's not real.

— *Redemption*

You've asked me to speak of eagles.
Of nocturnal flight over sunlit peaks.
To take your hand, guide you across clouds,
and illustrate the strength of God. I have. In you.

With faith, hope, and love under wing,
you have flown softly, quietly through me.
The embers of your saintly energy
raining down upon my soul. I weep.

Because *you*, my friend, are the eagle.
You see me.

-- Jason Sturner
(April Jellyfish Whispers)

warm dawn
waiting for wings to dry
the new monarch

> -- *André Surridge*
> *(March High Coupe)*

Exposed

For you
I spread my bones across the floor

arrange them in fractional patterns
and implore the gods to explain

why they won't break

why the assassins have
missed their mark.

Some of this matter
is held in our eyes

in the muscle of a
backward smile

it isn't that I take this breathing lightly
or miss the obvious pearls

that explode around me
like stars.

-- A.g. Synclair
(July Pyrokinection)

Penang

Asian flowers-Hypanthia and Fern-
mindful of coiled rain

of Mothers milk,

suckling fallow greens and blues
satiated by ancient hands-leavened spirits-
giver and taker of lives,

of heart and will,

bereft of everlasting *shi*,
the bereaved-lost and alone-
borne of fruit, and gum trees, and pearl.

-- A.g. Synclair
(July Jellyfish Whispers)

I Was Just Thinking

it's better to write alone
in a dark room
with a full bottle
and a heavy chest

even when it's all too much
the rain
the dark
the solitary thump of the heart

all of that
is better than suffering
her

because, clearly
she wanted me
dead

-- A.g. Synclair
(July Napalm and Novocain)

The River Always Captures Me

The Blue Line train crosses the river—
on one side the city,
the power plant, and rows
of brick houses, on the other,
the park with its paths
like veins of a broad leaf.
Below a tiny figure walks
a tinier dog. Someone else
bikes alone. No one rows
yet.

Soon the river will begin
to smell like spring.
More people will walk its paths.
Then it will reek like summer,
a regatta of rowers sweating,
dogs dripping,
tadpoles dying in
drying mud.
In fall, the leaves
will cover the ghosts
as the last rower skims past.

Still later the flat opaque water
will freeze in patches.
From the matching sky,
snow will fall
past the tiny figure
and the tinier dog
that trace the paths
that are like
veins of a leaf

by the river
below the Blue Line.

> *-- Marianne Szlyk*
> *(June Jellyfish Whispers)*

Marigold

No one will ever say to me
"it was so
beautiful
it hurt."

My red is not the red
of a carefully cultivated rose
against a white fence.

My orange is not the orange
of the lilies
crowding the base of a statue
of St. Francis of Assisi.

My petals are as stiff
as the plastic flowers
overflowing
in your mother's closet.

My scent is musty,
from the days before
air conditioning.

Nonetheless,
I
am
a flower.

-- Marianne Szlyk
(July Jellyfish Whispers)

Dialectic in Abeyance

With little direction from their teacher,
the children—boys in white shirts and blue shorts,
girls in white blouses and blue plaid jumpers,
both genders united by navy blue knee socks—
file tidily up the stone stairs, presumably into the sanctuary,
out of view of the heretic loitering across the street, in any case.

The children are being schooled in the intricacies of submission.
They will remember these outings: the break from the classroom,
these homilies and sermons, their own links in the chain of tradition.
They will remember the candles in daylight and, with eyes lowered,
the rhythm of call and response: knowing what to say when.
They will remember the palace of certainty shielding the unknowable.

Children of the uncertain or the unbelieving, on the other hand,
will have no such collective memory, reflects the heretic.
They will not have entered edifices constructed long ago to celebrate
a force unseen, to sing hymns to events that may not have happened,
all the while rejoicing in the flutter of the dark
that will soothe away the summer and the dust of doubt.

Even if they arrive here later in life,
children of the uncertain or the unbelieving will never have had
this foundation, the ease of assumed understanding.
They will have to work harder to master these arcana, to submit,
for they have not learned through precepts bequeathed by elders.
Their missteps in the labyrinth, along with their zeal, will be noted.

They may find themselves longing for the ways of their parents, the
mess of uncertainty and unbelieving. They may remember arguments
at the kitchen table, figures gesticulating on a soapbox, reason marshaled
to question authority, action direct with a placard or an editorial or
bodies. Perhaps he will see these children some day outside a lecture or
labor hall or a bathhouse, thought the heretic, turning finally away.

Briefly, they could swap stories from opposite sides of the heretical fence.

-- Yermiyahu Ahron Taub
(May Pyrokinection)

Viscosity

Viscosity is the
resistance of fluid to
eventual deformation by

shear or tensile stress.
Viscosity is due to
friction of opposing

parcels of fluid at
varied velocities.
Pressure is needed to

overcome the friction between
the layers and keep the
fluid moving.

Viscosity depends on
the size, shape, and
attraction between

particles. For example,
honey has a higher
viscosity than water.

A fluid with no
resistance to stress is
known as ideal or

inviscid fluid. This
explains so much about
my life. Am I honey or

am I inviscid?

-- Sarah Thursday
(September Pyrokinection)

Lies To Tell My Body

My bones are steel-heavy
as I walk the days with it
Pores on my skin ache
weighted by an iron-core earth
pulling me towards her
Down, she says, lay with me

My eyes can't see clear
turn skull-bound, sinking
pregnant with memory
The fibers in my muscles
weep at their loss of it
motion, forward, direction

The nuclei in my cells
pull and push against-toward
refusing to agree with you
Everyday, they keep forgetting
why I can't just dial the number
or drive 23 miles northwest

My arms know the exit-curves
(like the length of your limbs)
my feet know how many steps
(like the edge of your sheets)
I don't need my eyes to guide me
my hands, they know where

But my heart knows to stay
in my honey-thick atmosphere
Lock the windows and doors
breath it in, long breaths
circulating it, the new oxygen

Lie to my body, if need be until
I don't need to remember why

-- Sarah Thursday
(September Napalm and Novocain)

I Continue to Refuse the Role I am Given

after Low's "In the Drugs"

I am tasked with telling a story,
hiding a story, breathing a story
for which I am not the intended
recipient. I did not choose—story
sought me out, called me up, whispered
as I went about my business.
Never tell me that I self-selected.
It is a lie. Narratives shifting
to match me are never coincidental.
I stayed alive while all else died.
An angel and a demon sit with me.
The angel forgives with her eyelashes.
The demon never speaks.

-- Josette Torres
(May Pyrokinection)

puddles overflow
paved lots and streets and sidewalks –
rain and rain and rain

-- Chuck Von Nordheim
(February High Coupe)

skies utter lightning
streams use a whirr of water –
few hear such wisdom

-- *Chuck Von Nordheim*
(February High Coupe)

Affection

I'll always love her,
If we lived eternally
I would die for her.

-- Anthony Ward
(April High Coupe)

Playing On My Mind

"Did I tell you about the time I sneezed into a load of cocaine? I was with my girlfriend at this party thrown by one of her artist friends and they brought out this whole wad of cocaine. They were passing it around, and when it came to me I held it in my hands, just to take a look at it, I wasn't gonna...anyway, I sneezed all over it and it went everywhere. They went hysterical and I was in hysterics. I got a much better high than they ever did I can tell you."

He was describing a scene from Annie Hall. I'm not the biggest movie buff but I've seen one or two movies—so, evidently, had Bernie.

He used to tell us these stories and we would listen to them with great interest, not because we thought they were true, but because we couldn't help but be intrigued by the fact Bernie thought they were true.

Did he think they were? I remember the first time I met him, he told me the story of when he and three of his friends went off in search of a dead body. How they had to outrun a train and fend off some older boys with a gun he'd stolen from his father's cabinet. Of course I recognised what movie it was straight away.

"Stand by Me." I said. "I've seen it about a dozen times."

Bernie looked at me as if I had said something incomprehensible.

"Seen what?" he asked looking at me like the stranger I was.

"The movie, Stand by Me. That's..." I paused, uncertain of why this appeared awkward.

"Huh," he shrugged, and then went on to tell me about the time he ate fifty eggs.

There are people, I'm sure, that can convince themselves they have lived a life they have not lived. Most of us like to think we are something more than we are. Some have been there done that without having to prove it to anyone. There have been times I might confess to having put myself in a film, especially those staring Natalie Portman, or where I get to take out my angst on the worlds ignorant, but I wouldn't tell others these things as if they'd actually happened. We all like to indulge our fantasies and escape the mundane reality of our lives, but we don't expect to live there in reality. Not like Bernie.

Bernie had an antiquated look about him. A look that said he could have known Huckleberry Finn and we'd have believed him. When you spoke to him it was like going to one of those drive thru's where you speak into a box and you find yourself anticipating the delayed response, replying to you as if you weren't there—as if answering a memory.

He described the time when he was stood on top of a yellow truck screaming into the abyss, pouring with rain. I recognised the scene immediately, and before I could return from the thought, it had encapsulated me. I found myself standing on that truck too screaming into the abyss.

"That didn't happen! You're stealing my scenes. You can live in *your* movies as long they don't involve *her*." I said.

One day he told me a story so incredulous it could only have come from a movie. But I couldn't for the life of me figure out what that movie was. *What movie was it? Had I seen it?*

I found myself scouring the internet. Searching for new movies I hadn't seen, old movies I'd never heard of. I was determined to figure it out, as if trying to discern the reality, but nothing fit the description.

Did it actually happen? Was it actually real? What did it matter to me?

-- Anthony Ward
(January *Pound of Flash*)

Blue Sky Dolphins

One moment on mountain road
sparrows fly up and down
in front of the car's grill
like dolphins leaping
before a ship's bow
as I, the captain, navigate
wave after wave of washboard road
keeping eye on blue sky horizon.

-- Diane Webster
(January Jellyfish Whispers)

Late October Soybeans

As I drive to the store,
the hairy pods dangle,
arthritic fingers
awaiting the reaper.
The once-golden field
brown and leafless,
the stalks stand
like a tangled headgerow
of bones exhumed
from a mass grave,
and I check my list.

-- Eric A. Weil
(April Jellyfish Whispers)

Morris's Magnetic Literary StuffonMyCat Haiku

-- for his beloved Feather

sleep smooth moment

she is chocolate
I lick her languid beauty
in love's drunk rhythm

sordid worship

singing tongue music
I lathered her skin moaning
lie together love

Stradivarius
forest moon symphony

shadow spring vision
please whisper sweet cool nevers
luscious goddess fluff

*-- Kelley White
(July The Mind[less] Muse)*

today you gave me
roses and a nectarine--
still, i slept alone

-- Kelley White
(March High Coupe)

Variations

your leaves
fall
like soft braids,
unraveling
there, your frame freshly raped
by wind
half nude
thin, from a season of illness
your body is shifting
broken
your limbs obsessing,
wanting to be touched
by something nonviolent,
something without hands
deep, your need to feel yourself,
breathe—
there is a gallery of those
just like you
along the road
like prostitutes, adorned in the
colors of an emerging evening,
numerous, but extremely alone

-- Serena Wilcox
(January Jellyfish Whispers)

Burial

I'm exhaling an old mirage
ghost in the desert heat

a woman I loved
her see-through veils
flying in a gathering dust cloud

stripping in a whirl
teasing just out of my reach

wishing I could sleep
in the soft white sand of her breasts

these last days with her revenge
my bones disappearing with a mere wave of her hand

nibbling at my heart... like I tortured hers.

-- Stephen Jarrell Williams
(May Pyrokinection)

Desert Flowers

Driving
hours into the desert
spilling sun

dusty road wheeling into sand
wrenching spinning tires under
into a final lunge

car revving
heat vapors over the hood

turning the engine off
sighing with the windows down

finally
where I want to be

opening the door to
all the answers

walking barefoot
breathing easily

a loner, rebel,
thinker of how it should be

I squat on a soft mound
drawing a picture in the sand

others have been here
tortoise, lizard, snake

skin rags
clinging to skeletons

listening to
hoarse winds
telling me to dig my roots very deep.

-- Stephen Jarrell Williams
(April Jellyfish Whispers)

University Years

We were like pretty flowers between the rails,
we watched demagogues run rings round
language and us baying at them crying we
will tell you what is right as if we knew, hopscotch
playing for the hungry, cutting blood
in that socialist pledge, boy scout brigade
there was no grit to our show, just plenty of blow,
& night-time delusions, as the early hours bring
their scents - as I trotted out last-minute essay-jobs,
scraping up gleaned fragments into a patchwork
that really made no sense - but none of us Gods
saw the shopping arcade was grimy & full of drunks,
the sky not reflected in glory but miserable pools
of loneliness heaped up against the wall,
this was me the I who knew nothing better
than being ripped off by Soho whores, and begging
for love off the inner roads of darkness
from where streetwalkers drag you into stairwells
and pluck, chicken – but this was a later spiral
into the core, a continuation of what
is never finished, fathomless pit, bitter well.

-- Patrick Williamson
(May Pyrokinection)

Fishing in Silence

*

We launch out on a row boat
before the sun floats out of the lake.

Prayers begin of the unspoken,
fishing for something to say.

*

A drunk fisherman falls out
of the boat, into silence.

Divers in wet suits, splash backwards, wordless,

down blackness, thick with silence.
Weeks later, a body bobs up.

*

Bait in a bucket is punctuation –
leave that behind, we do not need it.

*

Fishing for what to say,
nothing is caught.

*

In the lake, the reflection of pines,
stillness of shadows,

the meditation of poems
drunk with caught fish.

But I tell you, there is nothing bigger
once you catch it.

> -- *Martin Willitts, Jr.*
> *(March Jellyfish Whispers)*

Silence is a frog
forgetting harmony
on closing night.

*-- Martin Willitts, Jr.
(January High Coupe)*

Springing Forward

Flakes of white plum blossoms
fall like snow onto our yard
taking me back to winter fields
lying still beside our house
as I waited to see Santa's sleigh appear.
I feel sifting snow creep up my sleeves
when frozen ruts
slipped me into cold banks.
I hear delicious crunchy sounds
when walking on thin iced mounds,
and recall the itch and sting of frozen ears.
I make a u-turn from my memories
and find spring spread across our lawn.

-- Cherise Wyneken
(May Jellyfish Whispers)

Airbrushing

Because I have the heart of a Luddite,
Rather than using the self-scanner,
I'm standing in the supermarket check-out line,
Waiting for the old woman in front of me
To finish laying out her coupons
As if they were Tarot cards.

Next to me a tabloid brags A SECOND CHANCE AT ROMANCE.
Below the headline, with their arms around each other, beam
A minor actress, airbrushed into beauty,
Seductive with health after a liver transplant,
And next to her, dwarfing her,
Her basketball playing boyfriend, who received a kidney
From a cousin he never knew he had.
Both thank God and their doctors and the donors.

And I think of a man I met in Barbados
Who, like the ancient Mariner, condensed his life into one story.
Years ago he received a call that his son from his first marriage
Was dying in a hospital two thousand miles away.
The young man with a troubled past
Had stolen a car, and when pulled over,
Swore to the police that he'd never return to prison;
So he placed a pistol to his head and fired.

The man was urged to hurry,
That the doctors were keeping the boy on life support
Until he could arrive.
But the man delayed more than a day,
Before his wife could convince him to see his estranged son.
When he finally arrived at the hospital
He made it as far as the corridor outside his son's room and stopped;
He couldn't bear to see what was behind the door.

The doctors said that was his decision; to them it didn't matter.
The time had passed for harvesting any usable organs

That might have given somebody else a second chance.
All they needed now was permission to turn off the machines;
And he didn't have to go any farther for that.

If he had to do it over again, he assured me,
He still wouldn't have gone in.
He didn't want that to be the final memory of his son.
He'd rather remember him as the athlete he could have been,
A successful man loved by a beautiful woman.

-- Ron Yazinski
(May Pyrokinection)

The Oculist's Patient

Rise and look around you . . .
ON A CLEAR DAY

-- Alan Jay Lerner

It was as if by flipping a lens
I witnessed the world in that phoropter –
clear as baby skin and crisp at the edges.
Like the veins in leaves were mountain streams.
Like a pubic hair was a tall pine.
Later we stood in the alley behind his shop,
smoking and smelling Chinese food,
with me trying to describe what happened –
the bestowal of a mystical gift
on an unworthy without forewarning.
Being a paid devotee of science, of course,
he would have nothing to do with numinosity.
I almost completely understood,
having been there myself before the exam.
Yet there were spirits all around
in perfectly pressed tuxedos, ballroom gowns.
The iris of a cat was an obsidian ring.
An orphaned hubcap a full autumn moon.

-- Tony Yeykal
(July Pyrokinection)

Black Hole

That was the moment of crushing,

lying sleepless in the cold
hour before dawn, afraid to ask
and yet not ask: you, curled
from my questioning touch,
silent.

Light bursting inward,
fading.

That was the beginning of it.

Now the shriveling
winds rip
the last leaves from the trees, and frosts blacken
the dahlias in our garden: I see
the world engraved
with cold, and still
no snow to soften the ice-keen
talons of the merciless hawk.

And what of you, Orion,
stretched out across this wintry sky?
Is not your virility
a mere illusion?
Has not the sword
stabbed
deep in your gut?

Like you, I am silent.

Somewhere in your frame,
the astronomers tell us,
atoms are falling
inwards,

inwards,
beyond the reach of comprehension,
their radiance hovering,
quivering,
imprisoned by implosion.

This dark space is all that binds us.

I await new constellations:

will you, Leo,
Virgo,
Serpens,
in slow procession,
help me bear the pall
of Orion's springtime burial?

I circle this horizon, accelerating
inward, yet centrifugal:
a temporary equilibrium, this balance
point of crisis, this moment
when the wavering will
must make its choice -
existence
or extinction.

-- Mantz Yorke
(December Pyrokinection)

The Lonely Stalk Their Front-Room Windows at Night

The lonely stalk their front-room windows at night,
watching snowflakes fall in streetlight shadows,
silent, a robe over their shoulders,
rolling prayers and pleas through the folds of their minds,
standing until weary legs say "please, please."
Eventually day, night, light, dark become the same,
days are lost, holidays missed,
the front-room window a smear of old dreams,
vanished conversation.
Even the feral cats slash by,
indifferent to the fingertip tap on the glass,
pausing only to piss yellow
into the cold white snow.

-- *Dana Yost*
(April Pyrokinection)

The Chinese Painter and the Viewer

between your brush tip
    and mountain top
you seek eternity in the blank
    while i am lost
among thick patches of ink.

-- Changming Yuan
(October Pyrokinection)

Disarmament

Your arms disarm me:
I won't sign a peace treaty
that ends wars of love.

-- Bänoo Zan
(January High Coupe)

the noun *dream*
a few bare letters
succumbing to fresh water

> *-- Ali Znaidi*
> *(January High Coupe)*

From The Editors

Killing for a Dream of Self-Preservation

In the night you dream of killing. Not in cold blood with malicious intent, but in self-defense you destroy friend and stranger -- equally. With knife or gun, or both. And confess it all to your father as you wrestle with blankets that wrap around you, revealing the knife you keep beneath your bed.

In the day, armed with a pen, you slay these haunting images. Terrified, you struggle to sort the knowledge from the elusive thoughts that stuff your pillow -- certain that determination will destroy your persecutors. Ink melds with blood, spilling forth in a breathing prose of death.

Yet the truth is never hidden. I can see it even now as I envy your troubled slumber. I admire your rebellious heart, fiercely pumping fear and pride, fueling the turmoil. I, who have no dreams, wish for someone to kiss. For bloodshed to ruffle my blankets. I am jealous of your strife -- your effort to continue living. The instinct for self-preservation I lack. The demons you choose to banish are the lost angels I long for. Restless uncertainty clouds your vision, distorting the image. Allowing you to curse the gift I see, so clearly, before you.

-- *A.J. Huffman*
(June Pyrokinection)

Walking with Birds

Their language of song and sounding drew me through
the fog. I followed – no, I flowed
with their foraging flutter. Soothed by the surf
and their surfacing chatter. We were one
on the sunlit shore. Feathered or not, we forgot
our flight. For a moment,
the sand sealing us in safety as we countered
its calming crests with our silent fleeting. Call
to the wind: arm and wing raised. A prayer
for peace. Startled,
the scene breaks. Scattering in several silhouettes
or free.

-- A.J. Huffman
(April Jellyfish Whispers)

Of Adverbs and Misguided Affairs

Reluctantly. I am speaking
backwards (against myself). You are
the embodied antonym for complacency,
compliancy and co-dependency.
And yet we play together so harmonically.
A symphony of sin and sun and silence
[laughing]. We are a communal
(of sorts). An undecyphered language
locked in lethargy. Hesitation seems to be
our Rosetta. (Motion our only road block.)
Statistically stasis should resolve
our burning [desire to resist]. Feelings
falter blindly between four hands and numerous
fingers pointlessly passing [nothing]
through nothing but layers and levels
of disillusioned dark.

-- A.J. Huffman
(February Napalm and Novocain)

Conversation with an Uncooked Egg

"To crack or not to crack,
that is the question."

                                          The egg remained stoic, white
                                          showed no signs of responsive
                                          movement.

I pondered this reticence in the face
of consumption, tried again to engage.
"Do you, in fact, pre-date infamous
chicken?'

                                          Nothing. Egg refused to even crack
                                          a smile.

I continued, alone in this diatribe.
"Is it wrong that I am okay with
cracking/frying/digesting you,
knowing that – were my intentions
swayed – you might have gone on
to hatch/grow/lay eggs of your own?"

                                          Egg held tough, conceded no display
                                          of emotion. My rantings, ignored.

I went for the jugular, more personal
with fatalistic undertones. "Do you have
a serving preference? Shall I scramble?
Turn you over, easy? Poach?"

                                          Not even a blink. Just blank
                                          resignation, silent strength.

Defeated by such a show of courage,
I forfeit. "You win." I replace
fragile orb in carton, move on to bacon
for a more self-indulgent solace.

                          -- *A.J. Huffman*
                          (March The Mind[less] Muse)

Firecrackers spark
fantasies of fire and flight
that linger like smoke.

Tiny hands applaud
thunderous booming followed
by a rain of light.

-- A.J. Huffman
(July High Coupe)

Shoveling the Trampoline

Who does this? is my first thought.
My second, *how cold IS it out here?*
I am rescuing my son's summer
pastime and therapy tool –
proprioceptive or vestibular sensory
input? I can never remember which –
from the weight of three day's snow.
The center is sagging, stretching
and will give out
if I do not. I am not
strong enough to lift
shovelfuls up
          and over
                    the top
of the protective enclosure.
Each scoop must be shoved through the entrance,
an unzipped hole more narrow than my blade.
Soon, I am not thinking at all,
one with the shovel, heaving
each clump into a growing pile below,
careful not to scrape bottom
and tear fragile, frozen nylon.

                    -- April Salzano
                    (April Pyrokinection)

Battle at the Birdfeeder

Blue jays are bastards,
deceptive in their coat of contrasts, the first
to be admired by those who have spent less
time observing their terrorist tactics.
But I'm on to them. I know their tricks: steer
the cardinals away from the corn, pretend
the suet tastes better, then dive
bomb. Strength does not come in numbers.
They hate indiscriminately. They are not working
as a team, but by lunch, ten cardinals
are losing to half as many jays.
Red blends with the remaining dead
leaves so that the cardinals look like decorations,
poised in defeat, waiting for leftovers.

-- April Salzano
(March Jellyfish Whispers)

The Real Story

I thought I had a story to tell
of quick death, of love
passing, of tragedy.
Eyes of a blue dog looked upon,
finally. Of finding and losing the one
person who knew me, who I could know
like a thought, completed, translated
into words at last, like the relief of dreams
that find their way into daylight, captured.
Of a bite not preceded by bark, what omniscience
failed to see. Of subliminal-
probably, unspoken as the breath
of heat made real, then consumed by its own
fire, burned alive. That was not my story.
Mine was one of survival, instinct
rather than will. Flight
rather than fight. Not territorial
pissing, but leaving a marked place
as far behind as my heart can allow.

-- April Salzano
(January Napalm and Novocain)

Choose to think he can,
or choose to think he cannot.
He will prove you right.

Pac Man, Mario,
noises that reverberate.
Rock, block, flap, jump, stim.

Same sentence over
and over stuck on repeat
comfort one more time

It's loud, I like it.
Too much is never enough
to fill my silence.

Developmental
delay. Axis II deferred.
Only time will tell.

-- April Salzano
(July High Coupe)

Assault by Baby

"Omg! This lady behind me in line at Starbucks just hit me with her baby!" I text my friend. This is one of those you're-so-not-going-to-believe-this messages. Such things are urgent, ephemeral, and often require an ignoring of the rules, such as signs that read *We will gladly take your order when you are finished with your phone call* with the picture of the only available picture of a cell phone in the click art program, the archaic flip phone inside a circle with a red diagonal line through it, indicating something serious like contraband.

If she's done it once, she's done it four more times by the time I get a reply: "what? like wielding her baby like a baseball bat and hitting you with it?"

"No, but that's damned funny too. This baby she's assaulting me with hasn't even been born yet. She's pregnant." I hit send then continue with a new message. "Obviously her depth perception is off. I mean, I know it's a hard load to bear and she probably can't even see her feet she's so big, but surely she can see me?! I'm waitin for my latte and she just.keeps.bumping.me with her damn baby!" Send. "I'm gettin pissed! I'm gonna slap her!"

"Let me get this straight. u are pissed at a fetus?"

"Lofl. Well, sorta. I mean, it's not the kid's fault its mother needs a decaf latte so bad she's willing to knock patrons out to get it."

"U sure she's gettin decaf?"

"Well, no. Should I ask her??"

"Eff that! She'll probably go into labor and you'll never get your latte. And you obviously need one if you are contemplating kicking a pregnant woman's ass."

"Good point. Ttyl."

-- April Salzano
(January Pound of Flash)

Author Bios

Shaquana Adams is an internationally published poet with a fondness for the color purple. Her poems can be found in Napalm and Novocain, Dead Snakes, Inkapture, Snow Island Review, Bicycle Review, Verse Land, and The World of Myth. She is quiet on the outside but goofy on the inside and writes because the best thing about writing is that she can say what she needs to say. It is an awesome experience.

Pamela Ahlen is program coordinator for Bookstock (Woodstock, Vermont), one of three Vermont literary festivals. She has organized literary readings for ILEAD (Institute for Lifelong Education at Dartmouth). Pam received an MFA in creative writing from Vermont College of Fine Arts. Her poems have most recently appeared in *Bloodroot, Birch Song, Bohemia* and *The Sow's Ear.* She is the author of the chapbook *Gather Every Little Thing* (Finishing Line Press).

Barbara Bald is a retired teacher, educational consultant and free-lance writer. Her poems have been published in a variety of anthologies: *The Other Side of Sorrow, The 2008* and *2010 Poets' Guide to New Hampshire, For Loving Precious Beast, Piscataqua Poems, Of Sun and Sand, The Widow's Handbook* and *In Gilded Frame Anthology.* They have appeared in *The Northern New England Review, Avocet, Off the Coast* and in multiple issues of The Poetry Society of New Hampshire's publication: *The Poets' Touchstone.* Her work has been recognized in both national and local contests including the Rochester Poet Laureate Contest, Lisbon's Fall Festival of Art Contest, Conway Library's Annual Contest, Goodwin Library's Annual Contest, and The Poetry Society of New Hampshire's National and Member Contests. Her recent full-length book is called *Drive-Through Window* and her new chapbook is entitled *Running on Empty*. Barb lives in Alton, NH with her cat Catcher, two Siamese Fighting fish and a tank of Hissing Cockroaches.

Mary Jo Balistreri has two books of poetry, *Joy in the Morning*, and *gathering the harvest*, both published by Bellowing Ark Press. A chapbook, *Best Brothers*, is forthcoming in spring, 2014 from Tiger's Eye Press. Mary Jo has published widely, and has three Pushcart nominations and two Best of the Net. She is a founding member of Grace River Poets, an outreach for schools, women's shelters, and churches. Please visit Mary Jo on her website maryjobalistreripoet.com

Alek Barkats is a second grade teacher in Washington, D.C. He has had poetry and fiction published in *48hour Magazine* and *Ostrenenie Magazine*.

James Bell has published two poetry collections *the just vanished place (2008)* and *fishing for beginners (2010)*, both from *tall-lighthouse*. He lives in Brittany where he contributes articles to an English language journal and continues to publish poems nationally and internationally with recent print appearances in *Tears In The Fence, Fire, The Journal, Elbow Room and Upstairs at Du Roc*. His latest eBook is *By Shinkansen to the Deep South (Poetry Super Highway 2013)*.

Jon Bennett is a Pushcart nominated poet and musician living in San Francisco's Chinatown neighborhood. His debut novel, speculative fiction about autism entitled *The Unfat*, will be coming out in April 2014. You can catch up with him on Facebook at https://www.facebook.com/jon.bennett.967.

Carly Berg is a heart-shaped box with a couple of chocolates gone. Her stories appear in over a hundred journals and anthologies. She welcomes visitors here: http://www.carlyberg.com/index.html

Joop Bersee was born in the Netherlands in 1958 in Aerdenhout. From 1989 to 1996 he lived in South Africa where he began writing poetry in English in 1991. His poetry has been published in South Africa, England, Wales, Canada, Brazil, India (in a translation),the United States and Ireland. In 2011 he was one of the winning poets of the Dalro Award in South Africa. Currently he works for the library of a museum in Amsterdam.

Abra Bertman lives in Amsterdam where she teaches English literature at the International School. Her poems have appeared in such journals as Stone Highway Review, The Citron Review, About Place Journal,

Other Poetry and Apeiron Review. She is also author of the poem "When the World Comes Home," which appears in the liner notes of the Jazz CD of the same name.

Shinjini Bhattacharjee holds an M.A degree in English Literature and is a self professed jabberwocky who loves to explore the poems garbed in emotions of varied hues every moment of her life composes. Her works have been published in, or are forthcoming in Metazen, Dead Flowers: A Poetry Rag, The Stray Branch, Nostrovia! Poetry,White Ash Literary Magazine, and Four and Twenty Poetry, among others.

Sara Bickley is a student at the University of Montana. Her poetry has recently appeared or is forthcoming in *Poetica Victorian*, *Trinacria*, and *Paper Crow*.

Brenton Booth resides in Sydney, Australia. Poetry and fiction of his has appeared in many small press publications, most recently Van Gogh's Ear, The Stray Branch, Regardless of Authority, The Kitchen Poet, Gutter Eloquence, Mad Swirl, Luciferous, Horror Sleaze Trash, Black Listed Magazine, and Boyslut.

Bob Brill is a retired computer programmer and digital artist. He is now devoting his energies to writing fiction and poetry. His novellas, short stories and more than 100 poems have appeared in over forty online magazines, print journals, and anthologies.

Michael H. Brownstein has been widely published. His latest works, *Firestorm: A Rendering of Torah* (http://booksonblog35.blogspot.com/) (Camel Saloon Books on Blogs) and The Katy Trail, Mid-Missori, 100F Outside and other poems (http://barometricpressures.blogspot.com/2013/07/the-katy-trail-mid-missouri-100f.html) (Barometric Pressures--A Kind of Hurricane Press). The Katy Trail, Mid-Missouri, 100F Outside And Other PoemsHis work has appeared in *The Café Review*, *American Letters and Commentary*, *Xavier Review*, *Hotel Amerika*, *Meridian Anthology of Contemporary Poetry*, *The Pacific Review*, and others. In addition, he has nine poetry chapbooks including *The Shooting Gallery* (Samidat Press, 1987), *Poems from the Body Bag* (Ommation Press, 1988), *A Period of Trees* (Snark Press, 2004), *What Stone Is* (Fractal Edge Press, 2005), and *I Was a Teacher Once* (Ten Page Press, 2011: (http://tenpagespress.wordpress.com/2011/03/27/i-was-a-teacher-once-by-michael-h-brownstein/). He is the editor of *First Poems from Viet Nam* (2011).

Candace Butler is a writer and artist living in her hometown of Sugar Grove, Virginia, a small town in the Appalachian Mountains. She is an MFA candidate at Antioch University of Los Angeles and is co-poetry editor of *Lunch Ticket*.

J.J. Campbell lives and writes on a farm in Brookville, Ohio. He's been widely published over the years, most recently at The Camel Saloon, ZYX, Dead Snakes, Regardless Of Authority, and Klar (Norway). His latest collection, *Sofisticated White Trash*, has received great reviews and is available wherever people buy books these days. You can find J.J. most days polluting the world with his thoughts on his blog, evil delights (http://evildelights.blogspot.com).

Theresa A. Cancro lives in Wilmington, Delaware, and writes poetry and fiction. Her poems have appeared, or are forthcoming, on several online sites and in print publications, including Three Line Poetry, Napalm and Novocain, Jellyfish Whispers, Pyrokinection, Kumquat Poetry, Storm Cloud Poets Anthology, Conversation with a Christmas Bulb Anthology, A Handful of Stones and A Hundred Gourds.

Valentina Cano is a student of classical singing who spends whatever free time either writing or reading. Her works have appeared in Exercise Bowler, Blinking Cursor, Theory Train, Cartier Street Press, Berg Gasse 19, Precious Metals, A Handful of Dust, The Scarlet Sound, The Adroit Journal, Perceptions Literary Magazine, Welcome to Wherever, The Corner Club Press, Death Rattle, Danse Macabre, Subliminal Interiors, Generations Literary Journal, A Narrow Fellow, Super Poetry Highway, Stream Press, Stone Telling, Popshot, Golden Sparrow Literary Review, Rem Magazine, Structo, The 22 Magazine, The Black Fox Literary Magazine, Niteblade, Tuck Magazine, Ontologica, Congruent Spaces Magazine, Pipe Dream, Decades

Review, Anatomy, Lowestof Chronicle, Muddy River Poetry Review, Lady Ink Magazine, Spark Anthology, Awaken Consciousness Magazine, Vine Leaves Literary Magazine, Avalon Literary Review, Caduceus, White Masquerade Anthology and Perhaps I'm Wrong About the World. Her poetry has been nominated for Best of the Web and the Pushcart Prize. You can find her here: http://carabosseslibrary.blogspot.com

Arthur Carey is a former newspaper reporter and journalism instructor who lives in the San Francisco Bay area. He is a member of the California Writers Club. His fiction has appeared in print and Internet publications, including Pedestal, Funny Times, Eclectic Flash, Writers' Journal, Golden Visions Magazine and Suspense. He is the author of "The Gender War," a humor novel available on Amazon. His most memorable moment as a journalist was racing into the pressroom after a picture had appeared upside down on page one and shouting "stop the presses!" No one heard him above the roar.

Fern G.Z. Carr is a lawyer, teacher and past president of the Society for the Prevention of Cruelty to Animals. A member of and former Poet-in-Residence for the League of Canadian Poets, she composes and translates poetry in five languages. Carr is a 2013 Pushcart Prize nominee and has been cited as a contributor to the Prakalpana literary movement in India. She has been published extensively world-wide from Finland to the Seychelles. Some of her poetry was assigned reading for a West Virginia University College of Law course entitled "Lawyers, Poets, and Poetry". Canadian honours include: an online feature in *The Globe and Mail,* Canada's national newspaper; poetry set to music by a Juno-nominated musician; and her poem, "I Am", chosen by the Parliamentary Poet Laureate as Poem of the Month for Canada. One of Carr's haiku is even included on a DVD sent to Mars on NASA's MAVEN spacecraft. www.ferngzcarr.com

J.R. Carson has multiple prose pieces in publications such as *Anathematic*, *Skive Magazine*, and *Defenestration*. His poetry can be found in *The Mind[less] Muse* and *Skive Magazine*. An award-winning playwright and poet, his poetry placed at the 2006 Sandhills Writers Conference and garnered him an invitation to Bread Loaf in 2007. In most of his work, he tries to tell at least three different stories from at least five different points of view, or whatever the cosmos may give him

Joseph James Cawein is a young poet from Southeastern Pennsylvania.

Christine Clarke lives in Seattle, Washington, where she divides her time between biology and poetry. She has been published in *DMQ Review, Clover, #4 & #5*; *Randomly Accessed Poetics, #4;* and *Gilded Frame – An Anthology.* Her poetry has received awards from the Seattle Public Library and Redmond Arts Council.

Mike Cluff is a writer living in the inland section of Southern California. He is now finishing two books of poetry: "The Initial Napoleon" and "Bulleted Meat" -- both of which are scheduled for publication in late 2013/early 2014. He believes that individuality is the touchstone of his life and pursues that ideal with passion and dedication to help the world improve with each passing instance .He also hopes to take up abstract painting in the next several months.

Martin Cohen is a retired computer programmer who loves dancing (favorites are West Coast Swing, Waltz, Foxtrot, and Salsa), writing poems, and solving math problems.

SuzAnne C. Cole holds an MA from Stanford, is a former college English instructor, and writes from a studio in the Texas Hill Country. Her flash fiction has been published in many anthologies and magazines including The World's Best Shortest Stories (of all time), has been listed on The Best of the Web del Sol , and nominated for Pushcart Prizes in both fiction and poetry. Her book *To Our Heart's Content: Meditations for Women Turning Fifty* was published by Contemporary. She's also published more than 400 essays, plays, and poetry in venues ranging from *Newsweek, Baltimore Sun, Houston Chronicle, San Antonio Express-News* to literary and commercial journals. She and her husband have traveled the world— Iceland, China, Nepal, Panama, Peru, Chile, Australia, New Zealand, Britain,

Ireland, Turkey, Slovakia, Costa Rica, France, Italy, Switzerland, and Russia. That being said, she also likes to imagine future worlds of exploration and imagination.

Corey Cook is the author of three chapbooks: *Rhododendron in a Time of War* (Scars Publications); *What to Do with a Dying Parakeet* (Pudding House Publications); and *Flock* (Origami Poems Project). His work has recently appeared or is forthcoming in *The Aurorean; bear creek haiku; Boston Literary Magazine; Cease, Cows; Columbia College Literary Review; Deep Water Literary Journal; Dewpoint Literary Journal; The Germ* and *Northern Cardinal Review.* Corey edits *The Orange Room Review* with his wife, Rachael. They live in Thetford Center, Vermont.

Larry Crist has lived in Seattle for the past 20 years and is originally from California, specifically Humboldt County. He has lived in Chicago, Houston, London, and Philadelphia where he attended Temple U receiving an MFA in theatre. He's been widely published. Some of his favorites are Pearl, Rattle, Slipstream, Evening Street Review, Dos Passos Review, Alimentum, Floating Bridge Press and Clover. Larry is publishing his first poetry collection in March '14, Undertow Overtures.

Philip Dacey is the recipient of three Pushcart prizes and the author of twelve books of poetry, most recently Gimme Five (2013), which won the Blue Light Press 2012 Book Award, and has written entire collections of poems about Gerard Manley Hopkins, Thomas Eakins, and New York City. A poem of his will appear in Scribner's Best American Poetry 2014. With David Jauss, he co-edited the anthology Strong Measures: Contemporary American Poetry in Traditional Forms (Harper & Row, 1986). The Room and the World: Essays on the Poet Stephen Dunn Syracuse U. Press, 2013) includes an essay by Dacey.

Susan Dale has had her poems and fiction published in Hurricane Press, Ken *Again, Penman Review, Inner Art Journal, Feathered Flounder, Garbanzo, and Hurricane Press. In 2007, she won the grand prize for poetry from Oneswan.

Cassandra Dallett occupies Oakland, CA. Cassandra writes of a counter culture childhood in Vermont and her ongoing adolescence in the San Francisco Bay Area. She has published in *Slip Stream, Sparkle and Blink, Hip Mama, The Chiron Review, Bleed Me A River, Ascent Aspirations, Criminal Class Review, Enizagam, The Delinquent and The Milvia Street Journal* among many others. Look for links and chapbooks on cassandradallett.com

Mohana Das is a poet by passion. Currently pursuing a degree in engineering, she is allured by all things creative, and abstract. Stars, colors, wildflowers, bees and butterflies are all her darlings. A Pushcart nominee, her poems have been published or are upcoming in a number of anthologies, Vayavya, The Brinks Gallery Cafe, vox poetica and Tuck Magazine.

William Davies, Jr. lives in a town surrounded by dairy farms. He has been happily married for thirty-eight years. His work has appeared in the Cortland Review, Bluepepper, The Wilderness House Review, Gloom Cupboard and many others.

Jim Davis has recently been nominated for Best of the Net consideration by *Lascaux Review*, has won the *Line Zero* Poetry Contest, *Eye on Life* Poetry Prize (2nd Place), was named Runner-Up for the Best Modern Poem by Chicago's *Journal of Modern Poetry*, and has received multiple Editor's Choice awards. His work has appeared in *Seneca Review, Whitefish Review, Blue Mesa Review, Poetry Quarterly*, and *Contemporary American Voices*, among others. His first chapbook, "Feel and Beat Again," will soon be available from *MiTe Press*, of which *Boston Literary Magazine* said: "Canny, brilliant and unerringly insightful, Jim Davis lives in a world where nothing is ordinary."

Jessica de Koninck is the author of one collection, *Repairs*. Her poems appear in a variety of literary journals and anthologies including *The Valparaiso Poetry Review*, the *Paterson Literary Review*, and *US 1 Worksheets*. A longtime resident of Montclair, New Jersey, and a former practicing attorney, she holds a B.A. from Brandeis and and M.F.A. from Stonecoast.

Darren C. Demaree is living in Columbus, Ohio with his wife and children. He is the author of "As We Refer To Our Bodies" (2013) and "Not For Art Nor Prayer" (2014), both collections are to be published by 8th House Publishing House. He is also the recipient of two Pushcart Prize nominations.

Andrea Janelle Dickens is from the Blue Ridge Mountains of Virginia and currently lives in Mesa, Arizona, where she teaches at Arizona State University. Her poems have appeared in New South Journal, The Found Poetry Review, Thin Air, and the Cobalt Review. She is also a beekeeper, gardener and ceramic artist in her spare time.

Jacob Dodson is a poet from Austin, TX. He wrote crappy poetry in high school and gradually got better. His work has appeared in Pank, High Coupe, Verbatim, The Legendary, Out of Print and elsewhere. He was the 2012 Head to Head Haiku national champion and a member of the Group Piece National Champion 2013 Neo Soul poetry slam team. Jacob was also the 2011 Austin Nerd Slam champion, the 2012 Mic Check! Erotic Slam Champion and has written and produced shows that appeared in FronteraFest's Best of Fest lineup.

Janet Doggett has a master's degree in creative writing from Texas Tech University and has had many creative nonfiction essays published in journals, most notably, So-to-Speak and Tangent. Also, she has published essays on websites such as Celiac.com and The New England Writer's Society. A poem, Death, Maybe? recently was published (#20) in Drown In My Own Fears. Three poems are to be published through scar publications in Down in the Dirt magazine in March 13, April 13 and May 13. In 2003, I won the best writing award as a graduate student at the Albuquerque Pop Culture Conference. I live in Massachusetts.

J.K. Durick is a writing teacher at the Community College of Vermont and an online writing tutor. His recent poems have appeared in *Write Rome, Black Mirror, Third Wednesday, Foliate Oak,* and *Orange Room.*

Ann Egan has won many literary awards which include Writers' Week Listowel Poetry Prizes; The Oki Prize. She has written one historical novel – Brigit of Kildare; and three poetry collections, the most recent: Telling Time. (Bradshaw Books) A widely acclaimed nature poet, her numerous writing residencies include Laois County Council; Kildare County Council; Writer-in-Schools; Writer-in-Prisons. Her poems, broadcast on RTE Radio are widely published in Ireland, USA, England, and Australia. In 2013, she completed a reading tour of France and Germany, courtesy of The Arts Council and Culture Ireland.

Neil Ellman writes from New Jersey, and has been nominated for the Pushcart Prize, Best of the Net, and the Rhysling Award. More than 900 of his poems, many of which are ekphrastic and written in response to works of modern and contemporary art, appear in print and online journals, anthologies and chapbooks throughout the world.

Kristina England resides in Worcester, Massachusetts. Her fiction and poetry is published or forthcoming at Gargoyle, New Verse News, The Story Shack, The Quotable, and other magazines. Her first collection of short stories will be published in the 2014 Poet's Haven Author Series.

Alexis Rhone Fancher is an L.A. based poet/photographer whose work can or soon will be found in *Rattle, Fjords Review, The MacGuffin, Deep Water Literary Journal, BoySlut, Carnival Lit Magazine, Luciferous, HighCoupe, H_NGM_N, Gutter Eloquence, GoodMen Project, Bare Hands, Poetry Super Highway, The Juice Bar, Poeticdiversity, Little Raven, Bukowski On Wry,* numerous anthologies, and elsewhere. Her photographs, published world-wide, include a spread in *HEArt Online,* and the covers of *Witness,* and *The Mas Tequila Review.* A member of Jack Grapes' L.A.Poets and Writers

Collective, Alexis was nominated for two Pushcart Prizes in 2013. She is poetry editor of Cultural Weekly. www.lapoetrix.com

Elysabeth Faslund lives in Theriot, La., is an international, professional poet, changing with the times, but not the place. She believes the things she did in childhood and beyond, have become the stuff of her poetry She became the Louisiana Writers Society's Grand Prize winner of 1968. She is poet who has been internationally published since seventeen, and holds the Epic of Gesar a major work of literature, out-distancing the Bible by centuries.

Jennifer Fauci graduated from Adelphi University with a degree in English Literature and Communications. She writes poetry, children's picture book stories and YA fiction. She recently published her first children's book, "A Present for You, A Present for Me," on Amazon.com for the holiday season. Jennifer's freelance work can be seen in The Latin Kitchen, The Patch, Newsday and local tribunes. Her creative writing can be seen in The Story Shack, Napalm & Novocain, and Pyrokinection. Jennifer's writing often reflects her mood, life obstacles, the current state of nature, and has a hidden moral meaning throughout the piece. She hopes to obtain her MFA in Creative Writing and Literature in the near future.

Zachary Fechter lives and writes in Southern California. He has been published in Poetry Quarterly Magazine and Kind of a Hurricane Press. He is a graduate of Roanoke College in Salem, Virginia.

Sharon Fedor has spent her professional career as teacher and mentor in Special Education, engaging students that are fascinating and unique, and promoting the joy of discovery. She writes poetry and fiction. Her work has been published in *Napalm and Novocain, Halfway Down the Stairs* and *Spellbound* (online), and in *Point Mass, Legends*, and *Conversation with a Christmas Bulb*. She is the second place winner of the 2014 Zero Bone Poetry Prize.

Joan Fishbein has had her work appear in *The New Verse News, The Origami Poems Project of Rhode Island, The Southern Poetry Anthology: Volume One, The Kennesaw Review, The Frequency Anthology, Poetica* and *Helicon Nine*. She has work forthcoming in *Hope Street*, a chapbook by nine New England Poets published by Main Street Rag.

Ryan Quinn Flanagan has published thirteen collections of poetry and one joint chapbook through various small presses. He is a Pushcart Prize nominee, and a 2010 Sundress Best of the Net finalist. His poetry has appeared in nearly a hundred online and print journals spanning five continents.

Sarah Flint lives in the West Country of the UK and for several years has written about diverse interests including gardening, cooking and climbing. At present she likes to write poetry . She enjoys playing with words and tries to put them in an interesting order.her poetry has been published by The Pygmy Giant, Message in a Bottle and she has been runner-up in the Mountaineering Council of Scotland poetry competition.

Kenyatta Jean-Paul Garcia is the author of What Do The Evergreens Know of Pining, Yawning on the Sands, This Sentimental Education and Enter the After-Garde. He was raised in Brooklyn, NY and has a degree Linguistics. He was a cook for over a decade and has studied several living and dead languages. His work has appeared in BlazeVOX, ditch, Eccolinguistics, Caliban Online, Ron Silliman's Blog and many others. Currently, he works overnights putting boxes on shelves and spends his days writing, reading and attempting to translate poetry for an upcoming book. He is also the editor of kjpgarcia.wordpress.com and altpoetics.wordpress.com.

Trina Gaynon has poems in the anthologies *Saint Peter's B-list: Contemporary Poems Inspired by the Saints, Obsession: Sestinas for the 21st Century, A Ritual to Read Together: Poems in Conversation with William Stafford, Phoenix Rising from the Ashes: Anthology of Sonnets of the Early Third Millennium, Bombshells and Knocking at the Door*, as well as numerous journals including *Natural Bridge,*

Reed and the final issue of *Runes*. Her chapbook *An Alphabet of Romance* is available from Finishing Line Press.

Jessica Gleason writes because Bukowski no longer can. Gleason has two published books, "Madison Murphy, Wisconsin Weirdo" and "Sundown on This Town". Her work can also be found in Nefarious Ballerina, Fickle Muses, Postcard Shorts, Misfits Miscellany, Citizens for Decent Literature and Verse Wisconsin. If you want to read more of her work, google her. She also, occasionally, likes to sleep in a Star Trek uniform and has mastered The Song of Time on her Ocarina.

Marilou Goodwin writes from Florida despite obstacles such as Husband, Little Girl, Little Boy, Foo the poodle, and Ogre the Boston Terrier. Also things like tivo, aerial dance, and high speed internet access. It's a wonder anything ever gets done.

Allison Grayhurst is a full member of the League of Canadian Poets. She has over 290 poems published in more than 175 international journals, magazines, and anthologies. Her book *Somewhere Falling* was published by Beach Holme Publishers, a Porcepic Book, in Vancouver in 1995. Since then she has published ten other books of poetry and four collections with Edge Unlimited Publishing. Prior to the publication *of Somewhere Falling* she had a poetry book published, *Common Dream*, and four chapbooks published by The Plowman. Her poetry chapbook *The River is Blind* was recently published by Ottawa publisher above/ground press December 2012. She lives in Toronto with family. She also sculpts, working with clay.

Ray Greenblatt has recently had his poetry published in: Abbey, Comstock Review, Ibbetson Street, New Laurel Review.

John Grey is an Australian born poet. Recently published in The Lyric, Vallum and the science fiction anthology, "The Kennedy Curse" with work upcoming in Bryant Literary Magazine, Natural Bridge, Southern California Review and the Oyez Review.

Tom Gribble is a poet, publisher and teacher. His work has appeared in *Chattahoocee Review, Puerto Del Sol, Hawai'i Review,* and others. Tom was awarded a fellowship from the Artist Trust/Washington State Arts Commission and the Associated Writing Programs Intro to Journals for poetry award.

John Grochalski is the author of The Noose Doesn't Get Any Looser After You Punch Out (Six Gallery Press 2008), Glass City (Low Ghost Press, 2010), In The Year of Everything Dying (Camel Saloon, 2012), and the forthcoming novel, The Librarian. Grochalski currently lives in Brooklyn, New York, where he constantly worries about the high cost of everything.

Judy Hall is a teacher of English and is an MFA candidate at William Paterson. She's been published in *Linguistic Erosion, Rose Red Review,Literary Orphans* and elsewhere. She's currently writing a novel about a mother raising her bipolar child, based on her own experiences. Her other work can be viewed at: http://judyhall.x10host.com/.

Marilyn Hammick writes (and reads) when travelling, during still moments at home in England and France, recalling a childhood in New Zealand and years living in Iran. Her poetry has been published in Prole, Camroc Press Review, In Gilded Frame, The Glasgow Review and by Mardibooks and Writers Abroad: they are forthcoming in The Eunioa Review. She tweets @trywords and blogs at http://glowwormcreative.blogspot.co.uk

Christopher Kenneth Hanson (ckhanson81) ckhanson81@gmail.com
http://sites.google.com/site/ckhanson81}
https://www.youtube.com/user/ckhanson81
https://sites.google.com/site/indieartsl/

Linnea Wortham Harper lives on the Oregon coast among blue heron, bufflehead ducks, and intertidal befuddlement. She was a finalist for the Bunchgrass Prize, and has had work published or forthcoming in CALYX, Pyrokinection, Napalm & Novacain, Pound of Flash, and Stealing Time, among others. Her first full-length collection, *Stones in*

Flight, will be published in 2014. You can hear her read at oregonpoeticvoices.com.

Jim Harrington began writing fiction in 2007 and has agonized over the form ever since. Jim's Six Questions For . . . blog (http://sixquestionsfor.blogspot.com/) provides editors and publishers a place to "tell it like it is." You can read more of his stories at http://jpharrington.blogspot.com.

Dawnell Harrison has been published in over 200 magazines and journals including The Endicott Review, The Journal, Fowl Feathered Review, Napalm and Novocain, Jellyfish Whispers, Danse Macabre, Mobius, Vox Poetica, The Tower Journal, Queen's Quarterly, and many others. Also, Dawnell has had 4 books of poetry published through reputable publishers titled Voyager, The maverick posse, The love death, and The fire behind my eyes. Furthermore, she possesses a BA from The University of Washington.

Rick Hartwell is a retired middle school (remember the hormonally-challenged?) English teacher living in Moreno Valley, California. He believes in the succinct, that the small becomes large; and, like the Transcendentalists and William Blake, that the instant contains eternity. Given his "druthers," if he's not writing, Rick would rather be still tailing plywood in a mill in Oregon. He can be reached at rdhartwell@gmail.com.

Tom Hatch paid his dues in the SoHo art scene way back when. He was awarded two NEA grants for sculpture back then. And taught at various colleges and universities in the NYC metro area in art (including Princeton and U of Penn. in Philly). He is a regular at The Camel Saloon and BoySlut. He had recently published at The Mind[less] Muse, Jellyfish Whispers, Napalm and Novocain and Dead Snakes among others. He lives in CT with a few farms up and down the road works in Manhattan. His train ride to and from NYC is his solace, study and den where it all begins and ends.

Damien Healy is from Dublin in Ireland but now lives in Osaka, Japan. He teaches English and writes textbooks for the Japanese tertiary market. He doesn't have much free time to read or write poetry, especially with a two year old son, but on those happy occasions when life is not so hectic he can be found reading many wonderful poetry journals from the four corners of the world. He was nominated for the Pushcart Prize 2013 and has been published in Jellyfish Whispers, Napalm and Novocain, The mind[less] Muse, Poetry 24, In other words Merida, The Ofi Press Mexico, Poetry Scotland's Open Mouse, Spinozablue and The Weekenders.

Ed Higgins has had his poems and short fiction appear in Pindeldyboz, Word Riot, Otoliths, Tattoo Highway, Foliate Oak and Blue Print Review, among others. He and his wife live on a small farm in Yamhill, OR, where they raise a menagerie of animals including two whippets, a manx barn cat (who doesn't care for the whippets), a flock of blue-green egg laying Araucana hens, and an alpaca named Machu-Picchu.

Ruth Hill was born and educated in upstate New York, and has traveled North America extensively. She is a Certified Design Engineer, dedicated tutor, and enjoys spoken word. She has won 1st prizes in *Gulf Coast Ethnic & Jazz Poetry, Heart Poetry, Lucidity, Poets for Human Rights,* and *Writers Rising Up!* Her work appears in the US: *California Quarterly, Connecticut River, Litchfield Review, Little Red Tree, New Millennium Writings, Ocean Magazine, Perfume River, Song of the San Joaquin.* In Canada: *Ascent Aspirations, filling Station, Fresh Ink, Royal City Anthology.* In the UK: *Decanto Fish, Forward Press, Frogmore Papers.* In Israel: *Cyclamens and Swords* and *Voices Israel.* Online: *About.com Poetry*permanent collections, *Apollo's Lyre, Detroit Writers Guild, Pyrokinection, Rose and Thorn,* and many more. *Little Red Tree* will publish her first full-length book in 2014. ruthhill@joiedevivregardens.ca

Kevin M. Hibshman has had poems published in numerous journals and magazines world-wide since 1990. In addition to editing his poetry magazine, FEARLESS, both on-line and in print for the past seventeen years, he has authored twenty chapbooks of poetry and prose. He received his BA in Liberal Arts in 2010 from Union Institute and University/vermont College. Future projects include novels and perhaps a play or two. Kevin lives in Pennsylvania with his partner William, an artist and their cat, Siouxsie.

H. Edgar Hix is a Santa clone who lives in Minneapolis with his wife, Julie, and their elves (seven cats and one dog). His poetic specialties are short poetry and Christian religious poetry. Hix is a lover of limericks and other short, humorous verse and has published several.

Lynn Hoffman has been a merchant seaman, teacher, chef and cab driver. He's published three novels, The Bachelor's Cat, Philadelphia Personal and bang-BANG. He's also written The New Short Course in Wine and The Short Course in Beer. Skyhorse Books just published a second, expanded edition of the beer book. A few years ago, he started writing poetry. In 2011 his poem, The Would-be Lepidopterist was nominated for a Pushcart Prize. His memoir of a funny year with cancer, Radiation Days will be published in March 2014. Most of the time he just loafs and fishes.

Sue Neufarth Howard is a Cincinnati native, published poet, visual artist, former business writer in marketing and sales training at DuBois Chemicals, retired. Graduate of Miami University, Oxford (Speech-Radio/TV) and UC Evening College (Associate in Art). Member, Greater Cincinnati Writers' League (GCWL) and Colerain Artists. Received Third Prize and/or Honorable Mention in several Ohio Poetry Day Contests since 1998. 1983 Poet Laureate for Clifton Heights/Fairview - Cincinnati Recreation Commission Neighborhood Poetry Contest. Poems published: In January, 2014 issue of Cattails online journal; Gilded Frame anthology, Kind of a Hurricane Press; Point Mass anthology, Kind of a Hurricane Press; the online journal High Coupe; online magazine AEQAI; the Journal of Kentucky Studies - 25th Anniversary Edition; the Mid-America Poetry Review; Nomad's Choir; The Incliner - Cincinnati Art Museum; the Creative Voices Anthology of the Institute for Learning in Retirement, City of Cincinnati; in several For a Better World - Poems on Peace and Justice by Greater Cincinnati Artists anthologies; and Poetic Hours Magazine, Carlton, England. Poetry chapbooks published on Lulu.com: TreeScapes, EarthWords, In and Out of the Blue Zoo.

Liz Hufford is a poet, essayist, and fiction writer residing in Phoenix, Arizona. Her poem "Living with Scorpions" will appear in the inaugural issue of 300 DAYS OF SUN. She is currently working on a young adult novel.

S.E. Ingraham continues to pen poems from Edmonton, Alberta on the 53rd parallel where she lives with the love of her life and their aging border-collie/wolf cross. Recently Ingraham took part in the Pulitzer Remix Project, writing a poem a day, for a month, based on Sinclair Lewis' 1926 award-winning novel, "Arrowsmith". This led to a semi-regular gig reading (and masthead inclusion) for the Found Poetry Review. She's also slated to co-host, in the upcoming year, at Creative Bloomings, a poetry site where poets of all levels are invited to post to weekly prompts, and explore their strengths. Ingraham has an ongoing relationship with Edmonton's Stroll of Poets, and the Edmonton Poetry Festival, both outlets for reading work aloud, and for maintaining a presence within the local poetic community. Ingraham's work has appeared or will soon; in print, on-line/or both, in the following publications: In Gilded Frame, Otis Nebula, Shot Glass, the Poetic Pinup Revue - Fairytales and Fantasies, Pyrokinection, Red Fez, Of Sun and Sand, and The Blackbird Sings. Her work may also be found on any of her blogs including these: http://thepoet-tree-house.blogspot.ca/ and, http://seingrahamsays.wordpress.com/ and, http://aleapingelephant.blogspot.ca/

Jason Irwin grew up in Dunkirk, NY and now lives in Pittsburgh, PA. "Watering the Dead," his first full-length collection, won the 2006/2007 Transcontinental Poetry Award and was published in 2008 by Pavement Saw Press. "Some Days It's A Love Story" won the 2005 Slipstream Press Chapbook Prize. His forthcoming chapbook "Where You Are" will be published by *Night Ballet Press* in 2014. www.jasonirwin.blogspot.com

M. J. Iuppa lives on a small farm near the shores of Lake Ontario. Her most recent poems have appeared in *Poetry East*, *The Chariton Review*, *Tar River Poetry*, *Blueline*, *The Prose Poem Project*, and *The Centrifugal Eye*, among other publications. Her most recent poetry chapbook is *As the Crow Flies* (Foothills Publishing, 2008), and her second full-length collection is *Within Reach* (Cherry Grove Collections, 2010). *Between Worlds*, a prose chapbook, was published by Foothills Publishing in May 2013. She is Writer-in-Residence and Director of the Visual and Performing Arts Minor program at St. John Fisher College in Rochester, New York.

Diane Jackman has had her poetry appear in magazines and anthologies, including The Rialto, Outposts and Words-Myth and a short story in "Story" (Happenstance Press). She was winner of the Liverpool Poetry Festival competition 2006. She wrote the libretto for "Pinocchio", for the Kings' Singers/LSO performed at The Barbican, has published seven children's books and many stories. She lives in Norfolk.

Miguel Jacq is a French-Australian poet. He lives in Melbourne, Australia where he runs (some say ruins) an I.T business. His work has been published by The Blue Hour Press, Dagda Publishing, Deep Water Literary Journal, Kind Of A Hurricane Press, The Poetry Jar,

Vox Poetica and Visible Ink. In 2013, he was shortlisted for the Australian Science Poetry Prize, and published two poetry collections 'Black Coat City' and 'Magnetics'. He is co-editor of the online literary journal, 'The Blue Hour Magazine'.

Bill Jansen lives in Forest Grove, Oregon, two blocks from the building where he was born in 1946. Recent work appeared in Gap-Toothed Madness and Asinine Poetry. In addition to a self published collection titled Soft Thorns, about 40 poems have been published in various ezines and journals.

Michel Lee Johnson lived ten years in Canada during the Vietnam era. Today he is a poet, freelance writer, photographer, and small business owner in Itasca, Illinois, who has been published in more than 750 small press magazines in twenty-five countries, he edits seven poetry sites. Michael has released The *Lost American: From Exile to Freedom (136 page book)*, several chapbooks Of his poetry, including *From Which Place the Morning Rises* and *Challenge of Night and Day, and Chicago Poems*. He also has over 67 poetry videos on YouTube. Links: http://poetryman.mysite.com/ http://www.lulu.com/spotlight/promomanusa *https://www.youtube.com/user/poetrymanusa/videos* http://bookstore.iuniverse.com/Products/SKU-000058168/The-Lost-American.aspx   http://www.amazon.com/The-Lost-American-Exile-Freedom/dp/0595460917

Ken L. Jones has been a professional writer for the past thirty plus years. He has published in practically every medium that a writer can appear in. Among his earliest and most noteworthy accomplishment was as a cartoonist of note whose scripts appeared in the titles of such major publishers as Disney Comics and Harvey Comics where he was a lead writer for The New Kids On The Block family of titles. In the last few years he has shifted his emphasis to writing speculative fiction and horror short stories as well as very well received poems of horror which have appeared many times in anthologies and online and which also resulted in his first solo book of poetry Bad Harvest and Other Poems which was released by Panic Press. He also recently had a poem published in Poised In Flight from Kind Of A Hurricane Press. In addition to all this he currently is constantly turning in new horror poems to George Wilhite's Long Intervals of Horrible Sanity blog which features regularly updated selections of his latest visions of terror. You can find it at the following link http://georgewilhite.blogspot.com/p/poetry-by-ken-l-jones.html. In spare moments he is also preparing several books of his non-horror poetry work for possible future publication.

Judith Katz is the Lead Teacher for Creative Writing at the Cooperative Arts and Humanities Magnet High School in New Haven, CT where her signature courses focus on writing poetry. Her work has been published in several print and online publications including Sending Our Condolences, The Yale New Haven Teacher's Institute, and will appear in the next issues of The New Sound and Tidal Basin Review. She is working on her first chapbook entitled Old Blessings for a New World.

Ryan Kauffman is a first-year MFA candidate at Northern Michigan University. His previous work has appeared in Mused: The Bella Online Literary Journal, The Western Online, The Fringe Magazine, Writing Raw, and Haiku Journal. He currently lives in Marquette, Michigan.

Claire Keyes is the author of two poetry collections: *The Question of Rapture* and the chapbook, *Rising and Falling*. Her poems and reviews have appeared most recently in *Literary Bohemian*, *Sugar Mule*, Oberon, C*rab Orchard Review and Blackbird.* She lives in Marblehead, Massachusetts and is Professor Emerita at Salem State University.

Yasmin Khan lives in Mumbai, India with her husband and three kids. Her poetry has been published in Grey Wolfe's Autumn Legends Anthology, The Haiku Journal, Poetry Quaterly, Mused Bella online. She takes inspiration from nature and life around her to write.

Maureen Kingston is an assistant editor at *The Centrifugal Eye.* Her poems and prose have appeared or are forthcoming in *Gargoyle, So to Speak, Stone Highway Review, Terrain.org* and *Verse Wisconsin.* A few of her recent prose pieces have been nominated for Best of the Net and Pushcart awards.

Steve Klepetar has received several nominations for the Pushcart Prize and Best of the Net. His most recent collections include *Speaking to the Field Mice* (Sweatshoppe Publications, 2013), *My Son Writes a Report on the Warsaw Ghetto* (Flutter Press, 2013) and *Return of the Bride of Frankenstein* (forthcoming from Kind of a Hurricane Press).

John Kross is an aspiring poet living and working In Dallas, TX. His poems have recently appeared in *Napalm and Novocain, The Mind[less] Muse, Pyrokinection* and the 2012 edition of *Storm*

Cycle. You can read more of John's work and interact with him as the poet "V" at Hello Poetry. www.hellopoetry.com/v/

Craig Kyzar is an award-winning journalist and international attorney. After graduating from NYU Law School and enjoying eight years of legal practice in Manhattan, Craig is now heavily involved in nonprofit work dedicated to enhancing children's literacy skills and connecting economically disadvantaged youth with a life-changing love of reading. Currently hard at work on his first two novels, Craig's versatile poetry, personal essays and fictional work have been featured in national and international publications, including *Recovering the Self, The WiFiles, Green Heritage News, Houston News Online*, the *Point Mass* anthology and the *Of Sun and Sand* anthology.

Heller Levinson lives in New York where he studies animal behavior. He has published in over a hundred journals and magazines. His publication, *Smelling Mary* (Howling Dog Press, 2008), was nominated for both the Pulitzer Prize and the Griffin Prize. Black Widow Press published his *from stone this running* in 2012. *Hinge Trio* was published by La Alameda Press in 2012. Forthcoming is Heller's *Wrack Lariat* slated for publication bly Black Widow Press, Fall 2014. Additionally, he is the originator of Hinge Theory.

Glenn Lyvers is a poet and author living in Virginia Beach, VA. Lyvers is currently the editor of Poetry Quarterly and several lessor known journals. He has won two annual poetry prizes, a Wolfson award in short fiction and is the recipient of several Pushcart Prize nominations. Lyvers most recent book, Burnt Umber, published by MLM is available on Amazon.com until it is sold out. Learn more about Glenn Lyvers by visiting his online blog www.glennlyvers.com.

David Macpherson prefers to let his work speak for itself.

Michael Magee has had his poems and plays produced on BBC radio and on KSER FM (Pacifica Radio). His first book, "Cinders of my Better Angels" was published in 2011 by MoonPath Press. His poems and songs were produced by Mel/Munro on their CD "Vaudeville." He traces his roots to his grandfather in vaudeville and his mother who played honky-tonk stride piano. He waits by the beach sand running through his looking glass.

Donal Mahoney has been nominated for Best of the Net and Pushcart prizes. He has had work published in a variety of print and electronic publications in North America, Europe, Asia and Africa. Some of his earliest work can be found at http://booksonblog12.blogspot.com/. Some of his current work can be found at http://eyeonlifemag.com/the-poetry-locksmith/donal-mahoney-poet.html#sthash.A1MWANJM.dpbs.

Ally Malinenko has been writing poems and stories for awhile now. Occasionally she gets things published. She is the author of The Wanting Bone (Six Gallery Press), the children's novel Lizzy Speare and the Cursed Tomb (Antenna Books) and This is Sarah, forthcoming from Bookfish Books.

Jacqueline Markowski is currently working on a compilation of short stories and a collection of poetry. Her poetry and short stories have appeared in numerous publications including *Cochlea/The Neovictorian, Permafrost Literary Journal, The Camel Saloon, Pyrokinection* and *Jellyfish Whispers*. Her work has been anthologized in "Backlit Barbell," "Storm Cycle" and "Point Mass" (Kind of a Hurricane Press). She is a Pushcart prize nominee and was awarded first place in poetry at The Sandhills Writers Conference.

Denny E. Marshall has had art and poetry published, some recently. He does have a personal website with previously published works. The web address is www.dennymarshall.com.

Alessandra Mascarin is an Italian lady of 23 currently living in Cornwall, UK. Her passion for the literary world ranges from poetry writing to foreign languages, an addiction that has led her to a career in Translation and a life of travel. She writes her works in Italian, English and Spanish, as she feels that in some way she belongs to the three of them. Her life wish is to never stop writing and keep on travelling to find inspiration, words and answers.

David McLean is from Wales but has lived in Sweden since 1987. He lives there with his dog, Oscar, and his computers. In addition to seven chapbooks, McLean is the author of four full-length poetry collections: CADAVER'S DANCE (Whistling Shade Press, 2008), PUSHING LEMMINGS (Erbacce Press, 2009), LAUGHING AT FUNERALS (Epic Rites Press, 2010) and NOBODY WANTS TO GO TO HEAVEN BUT EVERYBODY WANTS TO DIE (Oneiros Books, June 2013). His fifth full length collection THINGS THE DEAD SAY is now out with Oneiros Books (Feb 2014). His first novel HENRIETTA REMEMBERS is due fall 2014 from Unlikely Books. A sixth full full length poetry collection will be a selection of poems inspired by Gerturude Stein. His latest chapbook SHOUTING AT GHOSTS is now available from Grey Book Press. More information about McLean can be found at his blog http://mourningabortion.blogspot.com/

Joan McNerney has had her poetry included in numerous literary magazines such as Seven Circle Press, Dinner with the Muse, Blueline, Spectrum, three Bright Spring Press Anthologies and several Kind of A Hurricane Publications. She has been nominated three times for Best of the Net. Poet and Geek recognized her work as their best poem of 2013. Four of her books have been published by fine small literary presses and she has three e-book titles.

Jim Meirose has had his work appear in numerous journals, including the Fiddlehead, Witness, Alaska Quarterly review, and Xavier Review, and has been nominated for several awards. Two collections of his short work have been published and his novels, "Claire," "Monkey," and "Freddie Mason's Wake" are available from Amazon.

Karla Linn Merrifield is an eight-time Pushcart Prize nominee. She has had 400+ poems appear in dozens of publications. Among her ten published books are her latest,*Lithic Scatter and Other Poems* (Mercury Heartlink) and *Attaining Canopy: Amazon Poems* (FootHills Publishing). Visit her blog at http://karlalinn.blogspot.com.

Les Merton has always been interested in writing; he had his first short story published in the Manchester Evening News in 1968. He started to write more prolifically in 1995 and is the author of 20 books. His poetry has been published in over 120 UK magazines and in 15 different countries. In 2002 he became the founder editor of Poetry Cornwall / Bardhonyeth Kernow which is still going.

John Miatech has published three books of poetry, *Things to Hope For*, *Waiting for Thunder* and *What the Wind Says*. He currently is working on a new poetry collection, *Beyond the Fence*, due out in May, 2014. Miatech's work has appeared in *Anesthesia Review*, *BlazeVox*, *RiverSedge*, *Cellar Roots*, *Big River Poetry Review*, *Savasvati*, *Blue Lake Review*, *Northwest Review*, *the Scribbler* and Kind of a Hurricane Press. He received the poetry award at the San Francisco Literary Conference in 2012. John lives in Northern California, where he teaches high school. He grew up in Michigan.

Jane Miller is a writer of poetry and short fiction from Delaware. Her work has appeared or forthcoming in *In Gilded Cage, Connected: What Remains as We all Change, Wanderings,* and *Halfway Down the Stairs*. She was awarded a 2014 Individual Artist Fellowship as an emerging artist in poetry from the Delaware Division of the Arts.

James Mirarchi is a legal secretary who moonlights as a poet. In addition to his poetry collections, "Venison" and "Dervish," he has written and directed short films which have played festivals. His poetry has been anthologized and has appeared in Crack the Spine Literary Magazine, Poydras Review, gobbet (UK), Boyslut, Bluepepper (Australia), Orion headless, The Mind[less] Muse, Dead Snakes, UFO Gigolo, egg, The Recusant (UK), The Houston Literary Review, Subliminal Interiors Magazine, Bad Robot Poetry (UK), and Clockwise Cat.

Mark J. Mitchell studied writing at UC Santa Cruz under Raymond Carver, George Hitchcock and Barbara Hull. His work has appeared in various periodicals over the last thirty five years, as well as the anthologiesIt has also bee nominated for both Pushcart Prizes and The Best of the Net. *Good Poems, American Places, Hunger Enough, Retail Woes* and *Line Drives*. His chapbook, Three Visitors has recently been published by Negative Capability Press. *Artifacts and Relics*, another chapbook, is forthcoming from Folded Word and his novel, *Knight Prisoner*, was recently published by Vagabondage Press and a another novel, *A Book of Lost Songs,* is coming soon from Wild Child Publishing. He lives in San Francisco with his wife, the documentarian and filmmaker Joan Juster.

Suchoon Mo is a Korean War veteran and a retired academic living in the semiarid part of Colorado. His poems have appeared in a number of literary and cultural publications. His recent chap book, Frog Mantra, has been published by Accents Publishing of Lexington, Kentucky.

M.V. Montgomery is a professor at Life University in Atlanta. His fiction and poetry received seven nominations for Pushcart, Best of the Net, and Shirley Jackson awards last year.

Afzal Moolla lives and works in Johannesburg, South Africa. He is an amateur writer and does so for pleasure.

Bradley Morewood is a native of Brooklyn. He currently lives in Tampa where he enjoys writing, performing and recording his poetry to improvised music. His poetry has appeared in Wild River Review, Meridian Anthology of Contemporary Poetry, Blue Collar Review, Dream International Quarterly, Red Ochre Black and White, Solo Novo Wall Scrawls, Wild Violet, Jellyfish Whispers, Pyrokinection, and other publications. His chapbook "Where the Bangles Live" was published by invitation by St. Leo University.

Wilda Morris learned to love poetry at home, from her grandmother and mother. Her poems have appeared in numerous anthologies and in such periodicals as *Avocet, About Place Journal, Switched-on-Gutenberg, The Kref,* and *Encore*. Wilda Morris's Poetry Challenge provides a poetry contest for other poets each month. It can be found at http://wildamorris.blogspot.com/. Wilda lives in Bolingbrook, IL, and writes an occasional nature blog for *The Bolingbrook Patch*.

Erik Moshe is an aspiring lyricist from Hollywood, Florida who is currently working on a collection of poetry about the future of DARPA, robotics and artificial intelligence. He is also attending college for a degree in English. Find him at Thecentersphere.yolasite.com

Christina Murphy lives and writes in a 100 year-old Arts and Crafts style house along the Ohio River in the USA. Her poetry is an exploration of consciousness as subjective experience, and some of her most recent work appears in the journals *Boston Poetry Magazine, Wilderness House Review,* and *Pear Noir!* as well as in the anthology *Remaking Moby-Dick* edited by Trish Harris. Her work has been honored with nomination for the Pushcart Prize and the Best of Net anthology multiple times.

Tendai R. Mwanaka was born in Zimbabwe, in the remote eastern highlands district of Nyanga, in Mapfurira village. Left Nyanga for Chitungwiza city in 1994, and he started exploring writing that year, when he was barely twenty. His first book to be published, *Voices from exile*, a collection of poetry on Zimbabwe's political situation and exile in South Africa, by Lapwing publications, Ireland, *2010. KEYS IN THE RIVER: Notes from a Modern Chimurenga*, a novel of interlinked stories that deals with life in modern day Zimbabwe was published by Savant books and publications, USA 2012, found here; http://www.savantbooksandpublications.com/9780985250621.php. A book of creative non-fiction pieces, THE BLAME GAME, will be published by Langaa RPCIG(Cameroon 2013), a novel entitled, A DARK ENERGY will be published by Aignos publishing company(USA). He was nominated for the Pushcart twice, 2008, 2010, commended for the Dalro prize 2008. He was nominated and attended Caine African writing workshop, 2012. Published over 250 pieces of short stories, essays, memoirs, poems and visual art in over 150 magazines, journals, and anthologies in the following countries, the USA, UK, Canada, South Africa, Zimbabwe, India , Mexico, Kenya, Cameroon, Italy , Ghana, Uganda, France, Zambia, Nigeria, Spain, Romania, Cyprus, Australia and New Zealand.

Adam Natali traded his rock-star stretch pants for the looser-fitting slacks of a writer while simultaneously swapping his music-industry major for a writing degree at Columbia College, Chicago. Since graduating in 2006, his fiction has appeared in The Cynic, Short Story Me, Pound of Flash, Zest, and Bewildering Stories. Adam is currently working on an ode to penny dreadfuls with artist Michael Bricis. That project's journey is being chronicled at www.quietrebelpress.com.

Rees Nielsen has farmed stonefruit and grapes in California's San Joaquin Valley, two miles southwest of Selma, for 35 plus years. He has written poetry, prose and painted all of his life. After the passing of his wife Riina, he moved to Iowa to live closer to his grandchildren, Marshall and Adelaide Taylor. His poetry and prose has been published in numerous magazines both here and in the UK. In May two of his paintings and two lino cut prints have been accepted for publishing in the Paradise Review. You may sample more of Rees's art work at thehowlingquail.com.

ayaz daryl nielsen is husband, father, veteran, x-roughneck (as on oil rigs), x-hospice nurse, editor of print publication *bear creek haiku* (23+ years/115+ issues). His poetry's homes include *Lilliput Review, Yellow Mama, Verse Wisconsin, Shamrock* and *Shemom*. He has earned cherished awards, and, participated in anthologies. His poetry ensembles include *Concentric Penumbra's of the Heart* and *Tumbleweeds Still Tumbling* and has released a selection from 36 poets titled *The Bear Creek Anthology*. His beloved wife/poet Judith Partin-Nielsen, assistant Frosty, and! bearcreekhaiku.blogspot.com translate as *joie de vivre*.

Alex Nodopaka originated in Ukraine-Russia in 1940. Studied at the Ecole des Beaux Arts, Casablanca, Morocco. Full time author, artist in the USA. His interests in the visual arts and literature are widely multi-cultural. However, he considers his past irrelevant as he seeks new reincarnations in IFC movies if only for the duration of a wink.

Agholor Leonard Obiaderi lives in Nigeria. He loves poetry and crime novels though he has no criminal friends. He has been featured as poet of the week in *Poetry Super-Highway* and *Wild Violet Literary*

Magazine. His poems have been published in Storm Cycle Anthology of Kindofahurricane Press.

Timothy Ogene was born and raised in Nigeria. He is the author of a forthcoming collection of poems, *Subsurface Conditions* (Ediciones Camelot, 2014), and has completed his first novel, with published excerpts at *The Missing Slate* and *The Smoking Poet*. Shortlisted for the 2010 Arvon International Poetry Competition, his work has since appeared in *Stirring, Poetry Quarterly, Underground Voices, The Medulla Review, Mad Swirl, Blue Rock Review, Haggard and Halloo,* and other places. He is the current editor of *New Literati,* the New College journal at St. Edward's University.

Turk Oiseau has had a poem in Nightsbridge, in UK. He is not really Turkish, he is Macedonian but dark like a Turk. Turk Oiseau equals Turkish Bird, turquoise, right, like a peacock? He is hoping that catches on. He is a CPA by day but loves the Imagistes at night and especially loves Charlie Parker, another kind of bird, as well as his favorite American, H.D.

Loretta Oleck is a poet and creative artist whose work braids into many disciplines as her poetry and photography have been published or are forthcoming in publications including *Feminist Studies, Word Riot, High Coupe, Right Hand Pointing, Cultural Weekly, Commonline Journal, The Westchester Review, Cactus Heart, Black Lawrence Press, Picayune Magazine,* and many others. Her first poetry chapbook will be published by *A Hurricane Press*, and her performed poetry was filmed as part of the Public Poetry Series by Fjords Review. She has read all over New York including the *Hudson Valley Center for Contemporary Art.*

Mary Orovan is the author of "Green Rain" (Poets Wear Prada, 2008) available on Amazon.com. She has current or recent poems on line at 2River.org, Winter issue, and First Literary Review www.rulrul.4mg.com. Print journals include, "San

Pedro River Review", "Poetry East", and many other publications. She's been writing poetry for about 12 years.

Al Ortolani has had his poetry and reviews appear in journals such as *Prairie Schooner, Camroc Press Review, New Letters, The Quarterly, The Boston Literary Magazine, Poetry Bay* and the *New York Quarterly*. He has three books of poetry, *The Last Hippie of Camp 50* and *Finding the Edge,* published by Woodley Press at Washburn University and *Wren's House*, published by Coal City Press in Lawrence, Kansas. His newest collection,*Cooking Chili on the Day of the Dead*, will be published by Aldrich Press in 2013. He is an editor for *The Little Balkans Review* and works closely with the Kansas City Writer's Place.

Derek Osborne lives in eastern Pennsylvania. His work has appeared in Boston Literary, Bartleby-Snopes, The Linnet's Wings, Literary Orphans and many others. His serial novella, "Falling in Love with Rebecca Vasquez" is part of the Pure Slush 2014 Series. A stream of consciousness piece, "The Night" was recently nominated by Flash Frontier for a Pushcart. To read more or contact, visit: http://gertrudesflat.blogspot.com, or email at derekosborne1@gmail.com.

James Owens divides his time between Wabash, Ind., and Northern Ontario. Two books of his poems have been published: *An Hour is the Doorway* (Black Lawrence Press) and *Frost Lights a Thin Flame* (Mayapple Press). His poems, reviews, translations, and photographs have appeared widely in literary journals, including recent or upcoming publications in *The Cortland Review, The Cresset, Poetry Ireland,* and *The Chaffey Review*. He blogs at http://circumstanceandmagic.blogspot.com

Jeffrey Park has had his poetry appear most recently in *Danse Macabre, The Rainbow Journal, UFO Gigolo*, and the science fiction anthology *Just One More Step* from Horrified Press. A native of Baltimore, Jeffrey currently lives in Munich, Germany, where he works at a private secondary school. Links to all of his published work can be found at www.scribbles-and-dribbles.com.

Faith Paulsen has had her work appear in journals and collections including philly.com, *Apiary, Wild River Review, Literary Mama, Blast Furnace, Sprout, When Women Waken, Canoodaloodaling,* three "Cup of Comfort" collections, and four "Chicken Soup for the Soul" books and "In Gilded Frame." She lives in Norristown, PA.

Lisa Pellegrini resides in Warrington, PA. Her poetry has appeared in *Zouch Magazine, Downer Magazine, Dark Matter, The Rainbow Rose,* and *Misfits' Miscellany.* She has forthcoming work that will appear in *Bolts of Silk, Eunoia Review, The Rusty Nail, L'Allure des Mots, The Lascaux Review,* and *The Alarmist.* She was nominated for a 2015 Pushcart Prize, and I was also selected as a finalist in the 2014 Lascaux Review flash fiction contest.

Andrew Periale is an Emmy-nominated artist, and has toured throughout the US as an actor and puppeteer. He has been the editor of *Puppetry International* magazine for 29 years and has written many plays. His text for *L'Histoire du Soldat* premiered last year with the Chamber Orchestra of Philadelphia. His poetry has appeared in *Light Quarterly, Yellow Medicine Review, Entelechy International,* etc. A member of City Hall Poets (Portsmouth, NH), he also served for four years as the Poet Laureate of Rochester, NH. He has been teaching the creative writing workshop at Noble and Biddeford high schools and is the NH state coordinator for Poetry Out Loud. He lives in the woods with a slender wife and two fat cats.

Freya Pickard doesn't write about imaginary worlds; she writes about imaginative ones. These are worlds that could be real in a parallel universe or another time dimension. She does not promote escapism; instead she takes her readers into a refreshing place so that they return to their normal lives feeling strengthened and refreshed. Freya's first novel, Dragonscale Leggings, is a parody of the genre she loves best; fantasy. In it, she gently pokes fun at the Arthurian legends, the common concepts of dragon slayers and dragons and how they should (or shouldn't) behave. Freya runs a quarterly Newsletter which features serialised short stories about her main character from Dragonscale Leggings; Dracomagan. Her creativity also finds an outlet at her two blogs; dragonscale clippings and purehaiku.

Winston H. Plowes writes his words with two cats on a narrow boat on England's inland waterways. His compositions have been widely published, hopefully making people pause and ponder the magical details of life.

Perry L. Powell is a systems analyst who lives and writes near Atlanta, Georgia. His work has appeared or is forthcoming in *50 Haikus, A Handful of Stones, A Hundred Gourds, Atavic Poetry, Dead Snakes, Decades Review, Deep Water Literary Journal, Frogpond, Haiku Presence, Indigo Rising, Lucid Rhythms, Mobius The Journal of Social Change, Poetry Pacific, Prune Juice, Quantum Poetry Magazine, Ribbons, small stones, The Blue Hour, The Camel Saloon, The Credo, The Foliate Oak, The Heron's Nest, The Innisfree Poetry Journal, The Lyric, The Mind[less] Muse, The Rotary Dial, Turtle Island Quarterly, vox poetica,* and *Wolf Willow Journal.*

John Pursch lives in Tucson, Arizona. His work has been nominated for Best of the Net and has appeared in many literary journals. His most recent book, *Intunesia*, is available in paperback at http://www.lulu.com/spotlight/whiteskybooks. He's @johnpursch on Twitter and john.pursch on Facebook.

Jenny Qi is a writer and biomedical sciences PhD student in San Francisco. She writes regularly for *Synapse*. Her essays have also been featured in *Huffington Post* and *The Atlantic*, and she has published poems in various journals, including *the vanderbilt review, Tabula Rasa, Cactus Heart,* and *The Quotable*. Check out what she's up to at undercoveridealist.tumblr.com.

Stephen V. Ramey lives in beautiful New Castle, Pennsylvania, which used to rival Pittsburgh in industry. His work has appeared in various places, most recently *Cease, Cows*, Lucid Play's *Glass Eye Chandelier* anthology, and the *Catherine Refracted* anthology from Pure Slush Books. His collection of very short fictions, *Glass Animals*, was published in January by Pure Slush. Find him at http://www.stephenvramey.com.

Niall Rasputin lives on a houseboat in SE Louisiana. He is in love with the swamp, but often has secret trysts with the stars. He believes that laughter and song are the finest of all opiates. He writes his madnesses and passions down as a form of daily exorcism. He will never understand his own species, but will die trying. He is never wrong, because he refuses to know anything. He is 245 in dog years.

Chris Redfern love to write short stories and comic scripts. He's been published in a variety of magazines, books and comics, but can't quite afford to give up the day job yet. A middle aged father of three young boys and hailing from Tewkesbury, England, his website tells more of his adventures into writing:- http://www.aatwatchtower.com/

henry 7. reneau, jr. writes words in fire to wake the world ablaze & illuminated by courage that empathizes with all the awful moments: a freight train bearing down with warning that blazes from the heart, like a chambered bullet exploding inadvertently.

Laura Rojas is a 19 year old from Colombia, currently living in Toronto, Canada. Her work has appeared in online blogs, local zines, and an Anthology released via the Poetry Institute of Canada. Currently, Laura writes for local magazines, curates an arts and culture blog, edits a student-run zine, and avidly sells her hand-bound chapbooks at art markets around the city. She dreams of publishing her own book, saving the amazon rainforest, and owning a Corgi pup.

John Roth is a native Ohioan who says pop instead of soda. His poems have most recently appeared, or are still forthcoming, in *The Orange Room Review*, *The Eunoia Review*, *Gutter Eloquence*, and *Poetry Pacific,* among a few others.

Sy Roth comes riding in and then canters out. Oftentimes, the head is bowed by reality; other times, he is proud to have said something noteworthy.cRetired after forty-two years as teacher/school administrator, he now resides in Mount Sinai, far from Moses and the tablets. This has led him to find words for solace. He spends his time writing and playing his guitar. He has published in many online publications such as BlogNostics, Every Day Poets, The Weekender, The Squawk Back, Dead Snakes, Bitchin' Kitsch, Scapegoat Review, The Artistic Muse, Inclement, Napalm and Novocain, Euphemism, Humanimalz Literary Journal, Ascent Aspirations, Fowl Feathered Review, Vayavya, Wilderness House Journal, Aberration Labyrinth, Mindless(Muse), Em Dash, Subliminal Interiors, South Townsville Micropoetry Journal, The Penwood Review, The Rampallian, Vox Poetica, Clutching at Straws, Downer Magazine, Full of Crow, Abisinth Literary Review, Every Day Poems, Avalon Literary Review, Napalm and Novocaine, Wilderness House Literary Review, St. Elsewhere Journal, The Neglected Ratio, The Weekenders and Kerouac's Dog. One of his poems, *Forsaken Man*, was selected for Best of 2012 poems in *Storm Cycle*. Also selected Poet of the Month in Poetry Super Highway, September 2012. His work was also read at Palimpsest Poetry Festival in December 2012. He was named Poet of the Month for the month of February in BlogNostics.

Walter Ruhlmann works as an English teacher, edits mgversion2>datura and runs mgv2>publishing. His latest collections are Maore published by Lapwing Publications, UK, 2013 and Carmine Carnival published by Lazarus Media, USA, 2013 and The Loss through Flutter Press, USA, 2014. Coming up later: Crossing Puddles through Robocup Press, and Twelve Times Thirteen through Kind of a Hurricane Press. His blog http://thenightorchid.blogspot.fr/

Weldon Sandusky graduated from Texas Tech University in 1968-a B.A. in English. He then got an M.A. in English from the University of Wisconsin and a law degree (J.D. 1975) from the same school. Divorce followed as did commitment to , first, the private psychiatric hospital, Timberlawn, in Dallas, and , later, the State Mental Asylum in Terrell , Texas. Mr. Sandusky petitioned for *habeas corpus* claiming a conspiracy to unlawfully commit him existed in violation of his constitutional rights. Upon release, Weldon got a job at Exxon/Mobil where he worked twenty years as a cashier-nightman. During August, 2005he underwent open heart surgery at St. Paul's Hospital in Dallas and have since been declared totally disabled. He has coronary heart disease.

M. A. Schaffner has work recently published or forthcoming in *The Hollins Critic*, *Dagda*, *Pennsylvania Review*, *Gargoyle*, and *Boston Poetry*. Other writings include the poetry collection *The Good Opinion of Squirrels*, and the novel *War Boys*. Schaffner spends most days in Arlington, Virginia or the 19th century.

Carl Scharwath has been described by The Orlando Sentinel, Lake Healthy Living, Think Healthy and Mature Lifestyles Magazines as the "Running Poet." His passions include being a father/grandfather, competitive running, sprint triathlons and photography. (His art photography is featured in the Conclave Journal.) His work appears worldwide with over fifty published poems and five short stories. He was awarded "Best in Issue" in Haiku Reality Magazine and was recently selected as a featured poet in Ambrielrev. His first poetry book "Journey To Become Forgotten" was published by Kind of a Hurricane Press.

Ken Seide is the pen name of a resident of Newton, Mass. His poems have appeared in *Midstream*, *Poetica*, *New Vilna Review*, *Voices Israel*, *Ibbetson Street*, *Muddy River Poetry Review*, *SN Review*, *Kerem*, *Whistling Shade*, and *The Deronda Review*. His short stories have appeared in *Poetica* and *Cyclamens and Swords*.

Dr. Ehud Sela is a veterinarian; he owns an Animal Hospital in Margate, Florida. Dr. Sela writes both poetry and prose. His writings can be found online and in print.

Adreyo Sen is an MFA student at SUNY Stony Brook, hopes to become a full-time writer. He has been published in Danse Macabre and Jellyfish Whispers, amongst other magazines.

Rex Sexton is a Surrealist painter exhibiting in Philadelphia and Chicago. His latest novel "Paper Moon" received 5 stars from *ForeWord Reviews* and was described as *"refreshingly intense, unusual in its complexity, and disquieting in its revelations."* His latest book of stories and poems "Night Without Stars" also received 5 stars from *ForeWord Reviews*, which commented on the *"wild beauty"* and *"joy of this collection ... the prose rabid, people hustling to survive their circumstances ..."* Another recent collection of stories and poems "The Time Hotel" was described by *Kirkus Discoveries* as *"... a deeply thought-provoking ...compelling reading experience."* His short story "Holy Night" received an Eric Hoffer Award and was published in *Best New Writing 2007*. His poem "Gift Wrapped" was nominated for a 2013 Pushcart Prize by *Kind of a Hurricane Press*.

H. Alexander Shafer works as a contributing poetry editor for Arcadia Magazine, and as an English Composition professor at Oklahoma City Community College and Redlands Community College. His poetry and reviews can be found in *BlazeVox, Pyrokinection, The Rumpus, The Writing Disorder*, and elsewhere. Shafer received his MFA in Creative Writing from the University of Central Oklahoma in 2013. He lives in Oklahoma City.

Matthew Sharos is a Follet Fellow at Columbia College Chicago's MFA Poetry program. His poems have been published in *Decomp Magazine, Eratio, The Bakery*, and *Eunoia Review*.

Tom Sheehan served in 31st Infantry Regiment, Korea, 1951, and graduated Boston College, 1956. Poetry books include *This Rare Earth & Other Flights; Ah, Devon Unbowed* and *The Saugus Book*. He has 24 Pushcart nominations, 362 stories on *Rope and Wire Magazine*, work in *Rosebud Magazine (5), The Linnet's Wings (6), Ocean Magazine (8), Eastlit (4)* and many internet sites/print issues/anthologies. His work has been published in Romania, France, Ireland, England, Scotland, Italy, Thailand, China, Mexico, Canada, etc. His latest eBooks are *Murder at the Forum (an NHL mystery), Death of a Lottery Foe, Death by Punishment* and *An Accountable Death*, all in 2013 by Danse Macabre. Other eBooks at Amazon or B&N include the collections *Epic Cures* (with an Indie Award); *Brief Cases, Short Spans; A Collection of Friends* and *From the Quickening*. His newest eBooks from Milspeak Publishers are *Korean Echoes*, nominated for a

Distinguished Military Award, and *The Westering*, 2012, nominated for a National Book Award. Pocol Press will publish a new short story collection, *In the Garden of Long Shadows*, with 7 western collections in the cycle.

Kirby Snell is an MFA candidate in poetry at the University of North Carolina--Wilmington. Her work has appeared or is forthcoming in *Crab Orchard Review*, *Unsplendid*, *Measure*, *Think Journal*, and others.

Felino A. Soriano is a member of *The Southern Collective Experience*. He is the founding editor of the online endeavors *Counterexample Poetics* and *Differentia Press*. His writing finds foundation in created coöccurrences, predicated on his strong connection to various idioms of jazz music. His poetry has been nominated for the *Pushcart Prize* and *Best of the Net Anthology*, and appears in various online and print publications, with recent poetry collections including *Mathematics* (Nostrovia! Poetry, 2014), *Espials* (Fowlpox Press, 2014), and *watching what invents perception* (WISH Publications, 2013). He lives in California with his wife and family and is the director of supported living and independent living programs providing supports to adults with developmental disabilities. Links to his published and forthcoming poems, books, interviews, images, etc. can be found at www.felinoasoriano.info.

Dr. Smita Sriwastav is an M.B.B.S. doctor with a passion for poetry and literature. She has always expressed her innermost thoughts and sentiments through the medium of poetry. A feeling of inner tranquility and bliss captures her soul whenever she pens her verse. Nature has been the most inspiring force in molding the shape of her writings. She has published two books and has published poems in journals like the Rusty Nail (Rule of Survival)and Contemporary Literary Review India (spring lingers),four and twenty, Paradise Review, Literary Juice, Blast Furnace and many more and one of her poems "Unsaid Goodbyes" was published in an anthology called 'Inspired by Tagore' published by Sampad and British Council. She has written poetry all her life and aims to do so forever.

Melissa Steinle is a graduate of the University of Wisconsin and has her BA in English and her MS in English Studies. She's had letters published in "Rolling Stone" and "Milwaukee Magazine". She currently resides in Milwaukee, WI with her family.

Leilanie Stewart is a writer, poet and artist. Her work has appeared in dozens of print and online literary magazines in the UK and US. Apart from running creative writing workshops for teenagers in London, Leilanie writes and promotes her work and she reviews the work of other poets and writers. Her blog has been listed as a poetry resource at the Write Out Loud directory. She currently lives in London with her writer and poet husband, Joseph Robert. More about her writing can be found at www.leilaniestewart.wordpress.com

Emily Strauss has an M.A. in English, but is self-taught in poetry. Over 150 of her poems appear in dozens of online venues and in anthologies. The natural world is generally her framework; she often focuses on the tension between nature and humanity, using concrete images to illuminate the loss of meaning between them. She is a semi-retired teacher living in California.

Russell Streur is a resident of Johns Creek, Georgia. His poetry has been published widely in the United States, Europe and certain islands. He operates the world's original on-line poetry bar, The Camel Saloon (http://thecamelsaloon.blogspot.com/), and is the author of The Muse of Many Names (Poets Democracy, 2011) and Table of Discontents (Ten Pages Press, 2012). He is an avid photographer whose works have been selected for showing by the Atlanta Artists Center and other galleries.

Jason Sturner grew up along the Fox River in northern Illinois. Of his many jobs, those he most enjoyed were naturalist and botanist. His stories and poems have appeared in *Space and Time Magazine, Every Day Poets, Mad Swirl, Tryst,* and *Sein und Werden,* among others. He has also published three books of poetry (all available as free downloads via his website). He currently lives in Knoxville, Tennessee, near the Great Smoky Mountains. Website: www.jasonsturner.blogspot.com

André Surridge was Born in Hull, England. André lives in Hamilton, New Zealand. He has won several awards for haiku and tanka. His most recent being the inaugural Janice M. Bostok International Haiku Award, 2012.

A.g. Synclair is an unapologetic pessimist, rule breaker, and rebel without a clue. When he isn't editing The Montucky Review and serving on the editorial staff of The Bookends Review, he is drinking from glasses that are perpetually half empty and collaborating with his partner in crime, the artist and poet Heather Brager. Despite being extensively published around the globe, he flies under the radar. Deftly.

Marianne Szlyk is an associate professor at Montgomery College, Rockville, and a member of the D.C. Poetry Project. Her poems have appeared in Of Sun and Sand, [Insert Coin Here], What's Your Sign?, and Something's Brewing. Other poems have appeared in Jellyfish Whispers, Aberration Labyrinth, Linden Avenue Poetry Review, The Foliate Oak Literary Journal, and Walking Is Still Honest. "The River Always Captures Me" responds to Urban Wildlife on the Anacostia River, Daryl Wallace's film shown at the 2013 Environmental Film Festival in Washington, DC.

Yermiyahu Ahron Taub is the author of three books of poetry, Uncle Feygele (Plain View Press, 2011), What Stillness Illuminated/Vos shtilkayt hot baloykhtn (Parlor Press, 2008; Free Verse Editions series), and The Insatiable Psalm (Wind River Press, 2005). He was honored by the Museum of Jewish Heritage as one of New York's best emerging Jewish artists and has been nominated twice for a Pushcart Prize and twice for a Best of the Net award. Please visit his web site at www.yataub.net

Sarah Thursday is a music obsessed, Long Beach poetry advocate, editor of CadenceCollective.net, and teacher of 4th and 5th graders.She is honored to have forthcoming or been published in The Long Beach Union, The Atticus Review, East Jasmine Review, Ishaan Literary Review,Napalm and Novocain,

Mind[less] Muse, Pyrokinection, Something's Brewing Anthology, and Mayo Review. Her full length collection, All the Tiny Anchors, is in the works. Follow her at SarahThursday.com.

Josette Torres received her MFA in Creative Writing from Virginia Tech. She also holds a BA in English and Creative Writing from Purdue University. Her work has previously appeared in Ayris, The New Verse News, and 16 Blocks, and is forthcoming in Eunoia Review. She is the Writer in Residence at the Lyric Theatre in Blacksburg, Virginia.

Christine Tsen is a published poet and musician performing throughout New England. She attended Eastman School and the New England Conservatory of Music. Her poems are published in *THRUSH Poetry Journal, Vine Leaves Literary Review,* and *The Bark!,* among others. In her experience so much of poetry feels like music, and music like poetry ~ and to her one lights up the other! More: http://www.ChristineThomasTsen.com.

Chuck Von Nordheim has had his work recently appear in Brigham Young University's *Leading Edge* and Lourdes College's *The Tau*. He currently lives in a yellow house by a green river, but will soon exchange this color scheme for California gold and Coyote blue and black due to his acceptance into the MFA program at Calstate San Bernardino.

Anthony Ward tends to fidget with his thoughts in the hope of laying them to rest. He has managed to lay them in a number of literary magazines including *The Faircloth Review, The Pygmy Giant, Jellyfish Whispers, Turbulence, The Autumn Sound Review, Torrid Literature Journal* and *Crack the Spine,* amongst others.

Diane Webster feels rejuvenated by nature, and in turn she experiments with various twists of imagination to help her readers visualize what she has seen. Diane's work has appeared in The Hurricane Review, Illya's Honey, ken*again, and other print and online journals.

Eric A. Weil lives and teaches in Elizabeth City, North Carolina, on the edge of the Great Dismal Swamp. "Late October Soybeans" is in his new collection of anti-war poems, *Ten Years In*, which can be ordered at www.mainstreetrag.com/bookstore. He has two earlier chapbooks: *A Horse at the Hirshhorn* and *Returning from Mars*.

Laura Grace Weldon is the author of a poetry collection titled *Tending* (Aldrich Press, 2013) and *Free Range Learning* (Hohm Press, 2010) a handbook of natural learning. She's an editor and nonviolence educator who lives on Bit of Earth Farm with her family. She regularly writes about learning and mindfulness at lauragraceweldon.com/blog-2/, posts food-related sarcasm at www.facebook.com/SubversiveCooking, and mostly perfects the art of procrastination.

Mal Westcott writes from the Bitterroot Valley of western Montana. His poetry has appeared previously in print journals such as Fence, Mid-American Review, Redivider and Third Coast, as well as in the on-line journals Shit Creek Review and Now Culture. He has poems forthcoming in the anthology For Rhino In A Shrinking World.

Kelley White is a Pediatrician who worked in inner-city Philadelphia and now works in rural New Hampshire. Her poems have appeared in journals including *Exquisite Corpse, Rattle* and *JAMA*. Her most recent books are *TOXIC ENVIRONMENT* (Boston Poet Press) and *TWO BIRDS IN FLAME* (Beech River Books.) She received a 2008 PCA grant.

Serena Wilcox has literary work published and/or forthcoming in Ann Arbor Review, BlazeVox, Word Riot, Word for Word, Moon Milk Review, and many other publications. Her first collection of poetry, Sacred Parodies (Ziggurat Books International) was published in 2011. You can find out more about her at www.serenatome.blogspot.com.

Gabrielle Faith Williams lives and writes in Chicago. She has been published in Columbia Poetry Review and is also a 2013 Pushcart Prize nominee.

John Sibley Williams is the author of eight collections, most recently *Controlled Hallucinations* (FutureCycle Press, 2013). He is the winner of the HEART Poetry Award, and finalist for the Pushcart, Rumi, and The Pinch Poetry Prizes. John serves as editor of *The Inflectionist Review*, co-director of the Walt Whitman 150 project, and Board Member of the Friends of William Stafford. A few previous publishing credits include: *Third Coast, Nimrod International Journal, Inkwell, Cider Press Review, Bryant Literary Review, Cream City Review, RHINO,* and various anthologies. He lives in Portland, Oregon.

Stephen Jarrell Williams loves to write in the middle of the night with a grin and grimace and flame in his heart.

Patrick Williamson is an English poet and translator currently living near Paris. He has translated Tunisian poet Tahar Bekri and Quebecois poet Gilles Cyr. In 1995 and 2003, he was invited to the Festival International de Poésie at Trois-Rivières in Québec. He is the editor of *Quarante et un poètes de Grande-Bretagne* (Ecrits des Forges/Le Temps de Cerises, 2003) and editor and translator of *The Parley Tree, Poets from French-speaking Africa and the Arab World* (Arc Publications, 2012). Latest poetry collections: *Locked in, or out?*, Red Ceilings Press, and*Bacon, Bits, & Buriton*, Corrupt Press, both in 2011.

Martin Willitts, Jr. is a retired Librarian living in Syracuse, NY. His poems have appeared in Bitter Oleander, Blue Fifth, Conclave, Kind of a Hurricane, Comstock, Stone Canoe, and numerous others. Winner of the 2012 *William K. Hathaway Award* ; co-winner of the 2013 *Bill Holm Witness Poetry Contest*; winner of the 2013 *"Trees" Poetry Contest*; winner of the 2014 *Broadsided award*. He has 6 full-length collections including contest winner "Searching for What is Not There" (Hiraeth Press, 2013) and over 20 chapbooks including contest winner "William Blake, Not Blessed Angel But Restless Man" (Red Ochre Press, 2014). He has a forthcoming web book "A is for Aorta" with *A Kind Of Hurricane Press*.

Cherise Wyneken is a freelance writer whose prose & poetry have appeared in a variety of publications. Her book publications include: prose: *Round Trip, Freddie, Spaceship Lands in Africa, Stir—Fried Memories/* poetry: *Touchstones, Seeded Puffs, Old Haunts, Things Behind Things.* Plus a children's cassette. Her poem, "Borne Again," was nominated for the 2013 Pushcart Prize.

Robert Wynne earned his MFA in Creative Writing from Antioch University. A former co-editor of Cider Press Review, he has published 6 chapbooks, and 3 full-length books of poetry, the most recent being "Self-Portrait as Odysseus," published in 2011 by Tebot Bach Press. He's won numerous prizes, and his poetry has appeared in magazines and anthologies throughout North America. He lives in Burleson, TX with his wife and 2 rambunctious dogs.

Ron Yazinski is a retired English teacher who, with his wife Jeanne, lives in Winter Garden, Florida. His poems have appeared in many journals, including The Mulberry Poets and Writers Association, Strong Verse, The Bijou Review, The Edison Literary Review, Jones Av., Chantarelle's Notebook, Centrifugal Eye, amphibi.us, Nefarious Ballerina, The Talon, Amarillo Bay, The Write Room, Pulsar, Sunken Lines, Wilderness House, Blast Furnace, and The Houston Literary Review. He is also the author of the chapbook HOUSES: AN AMERICAN ZODIAC, and two volumes of poetry, SOUTH OF SCRANTON and KARAMAZOV POEMS.

Tony Yeykal My poems have appeared in Art World Quarterly, Blackheart Magazine, decomP Magazine and Emprise Review. I am a part-time distributor of medical goods to India, and have periodically granted myself long stretches of time to read, write, reflect and idle away the days. Two poets I esteem are Joseph Brodsky and Robert Creeley.

Mantz Yorke lives in Manchester, England. He has been a teacher and educational researcher. His poems have appeared in various places including the anthologies 'Of Sun and Sand', 'In

Gilded Frame', the 'Best of Manchester Poets' series, 'In Protest' and 'Ekphrastia Gone Wild', and the magazines Butcher's Dog and Revival.

Dana Yost was an award-winning daily newspaper editor for 29 years. He is the author of four books, and a two-time nominee for a Pushcart Prize in poetry. This is the second consecutive year his work has been selected for *Storm Cycle*. He lives in Forest City, Iowa.

Changming Yuan is an 8-time Pushcart nominee and author of *Chansons of a Chinaman* (2009) and *Landscaping* (2013) He grew up in rural China and currently tutors in Vancouver, where he co-edits *Poetry Pacific* with Allen Qing Yuan. Since mid-2005, Yuan's poetry has appeared in *Best Canadian Poetry (2009;12), BestNewPoemsOnline, London Magazine, Threepenny Review* and 819 other publications across 28 countries.

Ed Zahniser has a new book of poems AT BETTY'S RESTAURANT THOMAS SHEPHERD LOVES DANSKE DANDRIDGE AND THE SHEPHERDSTOWN SONNETS available on Lulu.com at "Bookstore" -- type "Zahniser" in search box. Designed by Heather Watson of Pernot and Tatlin, the book pays homage to poets Ted Berrigan and Danske Dandridge and to artist Joe Brainard. In March 2014 Ed completed an ekphrastic collaboration with artist and graphic designer Tom Taylor, WORDS AND IMAGES, 12 poems and 12 digital artworks. Ed's poems have appeared in four books, five chapbooks, nine anthologies, and over 150 publications and websites/blogs in the US and UK.

Bänoo Zan landed in Canada in 2010. In her country of origin, Iran, she used to teach English Literature at universities. She has published more than 80 poems, translations, biographies, and articles in print and online publications around the globe. Her book of poetry "Songs of Exile" will be published in 2016 by Guernica Editions. She is the editor and compiler of Scarlet Thistles: A Canadian Poetry Anthology by the Ontario Poetry Society. She hosts Shab-e She'r (Poetry Night) in Toronto and believes that her politics is her poetry.

Ali Znaidi lives in Redeyef, Tunisia where he teaches English. His work has appeared in *Mad Swirl*, *Stride Magazine*, *Red Fez*, *BlazeVox*,*Otoliths*, *streetcake*, & elsewhere. His debut poetry chapbook *Experimental Ruminations* was published in September 2012 by Fowlpox Press (Canada) which also published his haiku chapbook titled *Bye, Donna Summer!* in March 2014 . From time to time he blogs at – aliznaidi.blogspot.com and tweets at @AliZnaidi.

About The Editors

A.J. Huffman has published seven solo chapbooks and one joint chapbook through various small presses. Her eighth solo chapbook, *Drippings from a Painted Mind*, won the 2013 Two Wolves Chapbook Contest. She is a Pushcart Prize nominee, and her poetry, fiction, haiku, and photography have appeared in hundreds of national and international journals, including *Labletter, The James Dickey Review, Bone Orchard, EgoPHobia, Kritya, Offerta Speciale*, in which her work appeared in both English and Italian translation, and *Chrysanthemum,* in which her work appear in both English and German translation. She is also the founding editor of Kind of a Hurricane Press. www.kindofahurricanepress.com

April Salzano teaches college writing in Pennsylvania where she lives with her husband and two sons. Most recently, she was nominated for two Pushcart prizes and finished her first collection of poetry. She is working on a memoir on raising a child with autism. Her work has appeared in journals such as *Convergence, Ascent Aspirations, The Camel Saloon, Centrifugal Eye, Deadsnakes, Visceral Uterus, Salome, Poetry Quarterly, Writing Tomorrow* and *Rattle*. The author also serves as co-editor at Kind of a Hurricane Press.

Made in the USA
San Bernardino, CA
15 May 2014